I0058352

UP IN SMOKE

UP IN SMOKE

How the Retirement Crisis Shattered the American Dream

RICHARD L. DEPROSPO

Copyright © 2015 Richard L. DeProspo
All rights reserved.
ISBN-10: 0692420134
ISBN-13: 9780692420133

DEDICATION

This book is dedicated to those who embody a new American vision; a willingness to examine the issues facing our nation unburdened by political ideology. Within them lies our hope for the future.

CONTENTS

PREFACE

M y hope in writing this book is to raise the public consciousness about our next economic crisis, one of greater scale than the last. The issues and the solutions cross both party lines and political ideology. Unlike the financial crisis of 2008 that brought about the Great Recession, our current economic threats do not originate in the banking system, although that network, now consolidated in the hands of five far larger, too-big-to-fail banks may exacerbate its development. Rather, the crisis we now face has far broader economic underpinnings, rooted in unfavorable demographics, the vast under-saving of financial resources and the increasingly narrow concentration of wealth.

I wrote this book following a successful professional career of thirty-five years. As I sat in front of my computer and contemplated the date at which I might retire, I considered my resources: personal savings, the balance in my 401(k) account and social security benefits that I had accumulated throughout my working career. I projected a conservative level of annual investment income from these funds, including the gradual spend-down of the account balances. Of course, what can never be known in this type of planning is just how long these funds might be required to last. With advances in medicine over the past thirty years, longevity for Americans has been steadily growing. The number of Americans living past 100 years of age is expected to grow tenfold by 2050. That would mean that those born in the mid-1950s have something on the order of a ten times greater chance of living to 100 than those born one-hundred years ago today, or in the mid-1910s.

I considered my expenses in retirement and what sort of nest egg I would need to meet these expenses. People don't often think of future income in terms of its present value today. But as a finance professional I was trained to do so. The question I asked is what balance I would need to accumulate in my retirement account today, in order to produce the future annual income needed in retirement, adjusted for inflation and taxes. Try it. It's an eye-opener.

And you can take this sort of analysis quite a bit further. I was curious, for instance, what level of retirement account balance I would need simply to pay the future property taxes on our family home. Our taxes are now roughly $15,000 per year and, living in California, are subject to automatic annual escalation of 2%. Assuming in retirement we would continue to live in our home for another twenty years, I would need to set aside somewhere between $225,000 - $275,000 of our retirement balances (depending upon my investment assumption going forward) just to generate enough income to pay our annual property taxes.

Now property taxes are tax-deductible for federal and state income tax purposes, so this lowers the requirement considerably. But utilities, water, gas, electric, cable, telephone, internet are not. Our utilities generally run another $1,000 per month, or $12,000 per year. That's another $350,000 – 375,000 to be set aside from our retirement accounts1. Taken together, I would need to fund a retirement account of something on the order of $600,000, or approximately *six times the average retirement account balance* currently held by pre-retirees (age 55-65) just to pay property taxes and utilities, before considering food, clothing and other life essentials2. An eye-opener, indeed!

My Dad, and many of his generation faced an entirely different set of circumstances as he approached retirement. Having worked for a corporate employer for thirty-five years, he was given a scheduled date at which he would be eligible for retirement benefits and a fairly exact annual pension, or defined benefit, that the company had guaranteed to pay. Taken together with social security benefits, this pension income provided him and my Mom, a housewife, with a very comfortable retirement.

But for the most part, his generation, those born in the period 1920-1940 were the last to fund their retirement through private sector pensions. Yes, there was some transition and there are still private sector workers today who may avail themselves of corporate defined benefit plans, but for the most part,

---

1 Assuming a combined state and federal tax bracket of 34%.

2 The average 401(k)/IRA balance for pre-retirees for 2013 was $111,000, but only 50% of this cohort even has funded retirement accounts. The average for all pre-retirees, those with and without defined contribution retirement accounts is $14,500. This is explained in greater detail in Chapter One.

retirement funding was about to undergo a drastic change. There are also those employed in the public sector, where defined benefit pension plans are still the norm. But for the most part, for those workers who entered their careers in the late 1970s or 1980s, their retirement funding would soon be held hostage by Corporate America's rapid transition from defined benefit pension plans to 401(k) defined contribution plans and IRAs.

Suddenly, and with little fanfare, the enormous burden of future retirement funding for the Baby Boom generation had quietly shifted from the balance sheets of corporations to that of private citizens. Companies who were not nearly so nimble in jettisoning this responsibility, largely auto, airline and industrial companies with strong union representation, were often thrust into bankruptcy – a last desperate attempt to get out from under a demographic tidal wave.

All of my planning compelled me to research 401(k) and IRA plans a bit further. After all, I had been quite fortunate to have held a high paying professional position for thirty-five years. Not only that, but I had begun funding my IRA account at the earliest possible opportunity, did so at the maximum level of participation and with the diligence of never missing one year of contributions. Now, I grant you my investment decisions may not have always been optimal, but for private investors they seldom are. But now, approaching age sixty, to be gazing into the future with little certainty of a date at which I could afford retirement had me wondering. If my experience was such, with the career opportunities I had been given, what would the retirement plans of the average American look like?

At the same time, my work with state and local governments across the country gave me a significant window into the pension liabilities of public employee retirement plans. While benefits promised to employees by these plans are often ample and in many cases nowadays, highly generous, the financial resources of local governments to pay these promised benefits are in most cases, increasingly desperate. The recent bankruptcy filings of the cities of Detroit, Stockton and San Bernardino highlight the extent to which public employee pension liabilities threaten the future of many local governments.

So here we stand as a nation: corporations actively divesting employee pension liabilities through either bankruptcy, plan conversions or partial freezes; public employee retirement plans underfunded by an estimated *$4 trillion* nationally; Social Security, by the Social Security Administration's own forecasts to become insolvent by 2033 and private 401(k) and IRA accounts under-funded by a projected *$6 trillion*. How we got to this incredible and tragic place is a story of the epic failure of America to manage its retirement funding. Where it leads us is to the insolvency of an estimated 30 million current and future retirees, the bankrupting of numerous state and local governments and a future economic crisis to rival that of the Great Depression.

* * *

ONE

A Crisis in the Making

*Intergenerational Equity - to hold the natural and
cultural environment of the Earth in common
both with other members of the present generation
and with other generations, past and future*

*— Richard and Peggy Musgrave, Public
Finance Theory and Practice, 1973*

The evidence of the retirement system fraying is abundant. From well documented under-saving, to the social security system that is projected to run out of funds by 2033[1], America's retirement is on the ropes. From employer sponsored defined benefit plans that have thrown endless companies into bankruptcy, to the troubled public employee pension plans that threaten the solvency of major US cities, we have a serious retirement problem. Despite each of these programs failings, however, as desperate and troubled as they have become, they pale in comparison to our nation's greatest failure in systematic retirement planning, the 401(k).

As we will see, the 401(k) plan, IRAs and other defined contribution benefit plans, all relatively recent creations of Congress, were nothing more than an experiment in self-directed retirement planning, with speculative outcomes for retirees from their very inception. The widespread availability of defined contribution plans was engineered by Congress, not as a bipartisan measure of broad retirement policy, but rather as a quick fix to then current tax policy. But it wasn't long before corporations and the financial services industry saw the opportunities provided by these new retirement savings accounts. With the rapid corporate adoption of new 401(k) plans (and a corresponding off-loading of traditional defined benefit retirement plans) the 401(k) served as the ultimate vehicle to heap the precarious and inexhaustible societal burden of elderly care back on the employee (and thereby relieve the employer). Today with an estimated eighty-eight million participants[2], these accounts are by all measures a dismal failure.

The financial crisis of 2008 fully exposed the inherent vulnerabilities of the defined contribution plan, and its *dependence* on equity risk to produce the returns necessary to fund a secure retirement. In the years following the financial crisis, Americans openly joked that their "401(k)s" had quickly turned into "201ks" as the rapid decline in stock prices decimated the value of many a retirement account. Compounding this pain, the sluggish economic growth that followed the financial crisis, coupled with weak labor markets, served to strain families' ability to save and rebuild their retirement accounts.

Tracking just how much individuals have saved in IRA and 401(k) accounts is tricky business, due to the various measures used to report the data. Many sources, including brokerage firms and mutual fund companies report their data as a simple arithmetic mean: they add up the total balances in all IRA and 401(k) accounts they manage and divide by the number of people holding those accounts. Thus, the estimated $102 million that Mitt Romney is believed to hold in his IRA is averaged in with the $15,000 of the average middle class household. It's just not a meaningful number.

No slight to Mr. Romney's contribution to America's retirement savings, but for the data to be reported in a way that is of any value in understanding the current retirement savings plight, the "average" balance needs to be calculated on the basis of the median. To do this, of course, you simply line up all the account balances at a place like Fidelity from smallest to largest, and find the account in the precise middle by value, with exactly fifty percent of accounts holding greater balances and fifty percent holding lesser. This is the only reasonable measure of what the "average" American holds in the way of retirement assets.

While the median value of retirement assets has risen in recent years, according to recent data of the Federal Reserve Bank the portion of respondents who even owned a retirement account of any sort fell to *less than half,* continuing a downward trend that began in 2007. For those who are fortunate enough to *have* a 401(k) account, even with recent record gains in stock prices, the median balance of 401(k)/IRA accounts was just $59,000 in 2013[3],3. At a four percent recommended annual spending rate in retirement, an account of this size would produce (pre-tax) retirement income of less than $200 per month, or less than the average American family spends on groceries *each week.*

According to a 2015 study of the National Institute on Retirement Security, the average or median working family has virtually no retirement savings at all. When all households are considered, those owning and those without retirement accounts, the median retirement account balance (of total retirement savings) is $2,500. For those nearest retirement, aged 55-64, the median balance of retirement funds is only $14,500[4]. The median balance of financial assets held by pre-retirees outside of retirement accounts is only $12,500 (with this amount declining from $18,300 in 2010). Home equity adds only another $70,000[5].

In a 2014 survey of the Employee Benefit Research Institute, more than half of *current retirees* – people already in retirement - reported total savings and investments of less than $25,000. Sixty-six percent of retirees report total savings of less than $50,000[6]. Eighty-three percent of retirees reported

---

3 A 2014 study of 3.4 million investor defined contribution accounts of Vanguard showed a median investor balance of $31,396.

total savings of less than $250,000, a number that will scarcely cover expected Medicare out-of-pockets expenses, with nothing left over for costs of living[7]. Of pre-retirees, those age 55-64, nearly two–thirds of families report total retirement savings of less than one times their annual income[8] (the financial services industry recommends savings of roughly ten times annual income).

According to a recent poll by the Harris Organization, for those approaching retirement age, those between 45 and 64 years of age, one in four report no retirement savings at all (sadly, nearly the same percentage as that reported for those over age 65)[9]. Younger generations, at least for now, are in no better shape. In the same Harris survey, an amazing 32% of Gen Xers, aged 34-45, reported no personal savings whatsoever.

Retirement savings throughout America clearly suffered following the 2008 financial crisis. In fact, dis-savings of retirement accounts – people prematurely drawing funds out of 401(k) and IRA accounts - soared at an alarming rate. The IRS charges a mandatory 10% penalty on funds drawn out of a qualified IRA or 401(k) plan by individuals prior to age 59 ½. According to IRS records, Americans paid $5.8 billion in early retirement plan withdrawal penalties for tax year 2010 and another $5.7 billion in penalties for tax year 2011. This would imply that the total balance of funds *prematurely* withdrawn from 401(k) accounts in just those two years alone totaled $115 billion! In addition, by the end of 2013, greater than 20% of Americans eligible to do so had loans outstanding against their 401(k) balances[10]. These are fairly desperate financial measures to take, but for someone who might be unemployed with benefits about to lapse, pulling funds out of a retirement account may be the only option.

A recent study by Interest.com reported that while the target of annual retirement income to pre-retirement wages (or, the wage replacement ratio) is 70%, few Americans are achieving this benchmark. Based upon US Census data, their study reports that "nationwide, residents age 65 and older are living on a median income of $37,847, for a wage replacement ratio of 59.63%"[11].

We also now know that retirement savings are closely correlated with income. Of working age households, nearly forty million do not own any form of retirement account, neither IRA nor 401(k). Those that do own such accounts, however, have nearly 2.5 times the annual income of those workers who do not. Nearly 90% of the top quartile of American households by income hold some form of retirement account (either IRA, 401(k), 403(b) or 457(b)) but only 21% of the lowest quartile by income own such accounts[12].

Many young people and even pre-retirees tend to dismiss the grim state of their own retirement funding, believing that they will simply work forever. In fact, expectations of the age of personal retirement are rising, with 37% now indicating they plan to work past age sixty-five, versus just 14% in 1995. Interestingly, though, while Americans think of age sixty-five as the typical retirement age or that they might work well past this age, in practice, we retire much earlier than this, *a full four years earlier* on average. This data is supported by research of the Employment Benefit Research Institute that indicates despite what their intentions might have been, in practice, half of current retirees were *forced* to leave the workforce earlier than planned, due to health issues or layoffs. Perhaps equally telling of the new post-recession economy, while visions of early retirement – prior to age sixty-five – danced in the heads of nearly 50% of workers back in 1996, those dreams were squashed by 2013 with only 26% of respondents so indicating[13].

It's equally interesting that as retirement nears, a greater number of survey respondents report that they plan to retire later than age sixty-five. While 37% of those age 18-29 expect to retire early, only 16% of those aged 58-64 plan to do so. Conversely, the number of respondents who expect to work past sixty-five rises with age, with greater than 51% of 58-64 year olds reporting this to be their current plan.

Whether the underfunding of defined contribution retirement accounts is the result of bad decision making, or simply the fact that for many families incomes were squeezed too low for too long to permit regular 401(k) contributions, the data on this one point is crystal clear. Of Americans offered a 401(k) plan through their employers, on average, fully 21% chose not to participate[14]. These individuals are perhaps confusing their *lack of desire* to participate with the unwavering *need* to participate in a retirement plan. This fact points to yet another failing of the modern defined contribution plan: it's voluntary.

The reason most often cited for workers' failure to contribute to 401(k) plans is that they simply don't have the money. Greater than 40% of workers covered by defined contribution plans cite the high cost of living and monthly household expenses as the top reasons for not contributing to their employer's 401(k) plan[15]. Given the lackluster growth in the economy following the financial crisis and the stagnation of real median family incomes going back to 1989, their argument, however desperate and unfortunate, may well be valid.

Moreover, for millenniums in their twenties who have changed jobs, 44% cashed out part or all of their 401(k) accounts, as do 38% of those in their thirties. And this phenomena is not limited to millenniums. Data show that 42% of those aged 40-49 and 26% of those aged 50-59 also cashed out their retirement accounts when changing jobs, with the percentages increasing across all age categories for those at lower income levels[16].

According to a report of the Federal Reserve Bank, only half of American households even have a 401(k)/IRA account of any balance; the rest, or an estimated 35% of Americans over age sixty-five, rely solely on Social Security, a topic we will discuss in Chapter Two[17]. Today, for the roughly fifty percent of those nearing retirement who hold 401(k)/IRA accounts, the average combined balance is only $111,000, having *declined* an average 8% from 2010[18]. Directionally the data indicate that retirement savings are falling.

But aside from the rate of savings, or the level of assets that Americans have or have not accumulated in 401(k) and IRA accounts, it turns out the 401(k) plan, quickly latched onto by Corporate America, was nothing more than a whimsical experiment in tax policy and one, as we will show, with critical design flaws. But what may have begun as a whiteboard project of congressional staffers with insufficient planning, analysis or forethought, soon held out great promise for American employers who were buckling under the burden of escalating pension liabilities. Interestingly, this trend away from corporate defined benefit retirement plans proceeded quite quickly, despite the fact that the National Institute on Retirement Security reports, "rates of poverty among older households without defined benefit pension income were approximately *nine times* greater than rates among households with defined pension benefits"[19]. Washington was apparently not listening.

The 401(k) also promised great reward for the financial services industry that quickly saw the creation of new IRA and 401(k) accounts as a fee bonanza for the investment business. According to the Investment Company Institute, 401(k) plan assets quickly grew to $144 billion by 1995 and to $2.4 trillion by 2005. The industry doesn't break out its fees for IRAs, 401(k)s or other plan assets, but a Bloomberg News poll in 2008 estimated the total annual fee income for the financial services industry from 401(k) plan assets to be close to $90 billion, with large players in the industry like the Principal Financial Group earning in excess of $300 million per year[20].

While the 401(k) proved to be something of a life raft for Corporate America drowning in pension liabilities it evolved into a disastrous lab trial for an entire generation of American workers. It turns out that even if you made the maximum contribution to your plan as provided under IRS regulations, did so in each and every year, made those contributions consistently for thirty years, never spent a day of your working life unemployed, made investment decisions for the assets with optimal foresight and waited until 65 to retire, you will almost certainly outlive your money. And for those not contributing the maximum, skipping a few years, or making less than perfect investment decisions - as most of us will invariably do - the outcomes are nothing short of disaster.

Retirement planning is not simply a personal issue, despite wittingly or otherwise Congress' best efforts to try to make it such through the creation of the 401(k). Retirement is a societal issue as well, unless we are willing to live in a culture of widespread elderly poverty. With the under-funding of imminent retirement costs having been estimated from *six to eleven trillion dollars*[21], and with an ever-growing number of retirement age voters demanding action, retirement savings may also soon become one of the defining issues of American politics.

At the same time that retirement expenses are projected to grow dramatically, the diminished spending of an aging society – particularly one so under-funded in its retirement savings – poses great challenges for American economic growth. These factors will conspire to reduce not only consumption, but also savings and, therefore, investment. Spending by the average consumer, it turns out, peaks at age forty-five[22]. By that age, consumers have already invested in homes, furnishings and the education of their children. Thereafter, they tend to significantly moderate their spending. And, unfortunately, that trend continues throughout their remaining years. Overlay a U.S. population curve by age, over this life-cycle spending pattern and you begin to understand how significantly consumer spending can decline in an aging society.

Accompanying this shift to an older society, amidst sharply declining fertility rates, is a falling off of working-age populations, not just in America, but globally. The working-age population worldwide is expected to grow *half as fast* through 2030 as it did in the preceding fifteen years[23]. This demographic consideration is already having profound implications for retirement funding in nearly all developed economies around the world.

There are now five advanced nations of the world economy that are classified as "super-aged" societies. Japan tops the list with 26% of its current population aged sixty-five and older, but Germany and Italy at 21%, are close behind. Each are projected to grow older through 2030. By that year, the total of super-aged societies will grow from five to thirty-four, to include the US as well[24]. With greater aging, reduced savings or dis-savings is unavoidable, as is reduced consumption for the great majority of these seniors. The combination of these factors will serve as a significant headwind to GDP growth, both here and around the developed world, through 2030.

* * *

J ust as personal savings for retirement are grossly underfunded, corporate-sponsored defined benefit pension plans of the largest one hundred US companies are estimated to be underfunded to the tune of $382 billion[25]. But it's the massive retirement liabilities of the public employee retirement systems of cities, states and counties throughout the US that are in many cases an outright disaster. The State of California will spend $45 billion this year on pension related costs alone, an amount equal to nearly one-half of its total indebtedness for capital investments in infrastructure, public health, the judicial systems, prisons and transportation. Despite this staggering outlay of public funds, the state faces an *unfunded* liability to its retirement system of $200 billion, an amount that continues to grow each year. The State of Illinois faces a deficit in its public employee retirement system of a staggering four and one-half times the size of its general fund tax revenue. To these massive burdens of states get added the local government liabilities of the cities of Detroit, Chicago, Philadelphia and many others, equally out of balance in the funding of their future pension expense.

What should be obvious, but what many people simply do not realize is that state and local governments rely upon taxes *from individuals* for the vast majority of the revenue that they raise. Be they personal income taxes, sales taxes, property taxes, motor vehicle license or fuel taxes, or taxes on services like utilities, telephone, or otherwise, the individual tax payer provides an estimated 91% of state and local tax revenue, nationally[26]. Faced with a shortage of funds necessary to pay any component of their annual general fund budget local governments, unless otherwise specifically limited by law, will seek to raise *tax rates* as the primary tool in addressing budget imbalances.

While 70% of those polled in a recent survey by the Reason Foundation indicated that they would oppose reducing benefits to public sector retirees, this same group also opposed raising taxes to pay for benefits[27]. Those polled were against raising taxes, against reducing government services, and against reducing pensions for retired workers (while being fairly evenly split on reducing pensions for current government workers). This failure to appreciate the linkage between local government liabilities and the tools by which governments fund these liabilities, is a primary obstacle in addressing the growing and unsustainable public sector pension crisis.

Taken in total from all sectors, public, private, corporate and individual, what we now see is a retirement landscape in great jeopardy. The federal social security system is perilously close to insolvency. Personal retirement accounts are severely underfunded. Private company retirement plans suffer imbalances, while public employee pension systems are staggering under the crushing weight of future liabilities. And most unfortunately, the day of reckoning of America's growing retirement crisis may be far sooner than any of us would like to believe.

*   *   *

TWO

"I'M WITH THE GOVERNMENT, I'M HERE TO HELP"

Retirement funding is still a relatively new concept in America. Prior to the adoption of the Social Security Act, and for the generations that preceded it, retirements were largely a function of personal savings. In fact, for the generations reaching retirement age prior to the Great Depression, no federal safety net for the retirement of the average worker even existed[4]. For most workers, that is the 85-90% not covered by employer-sponsored pension plans retirement as we now know it, simply was not possible. People ran businesses, worked in factories and generally did so until they no longer could.

---

4 The one exception would be military pensions, first adopted in 1862 in America as the Civil War Pension program, a program designed to provide care of widows, orphans and disabled veterans of the Civil War. The program provided widows and orphans pensions in an amount equal to their deceased soldier, had he been disabled. Through modifications in the years that followed, by 1910, any Civil War veteran and survivors were paid disability, old-age and survivors benefits, much like the later to be offered Social Security System.

They then relied upon the support of children or personal savings to live out their remaining years. The Social Security Act changed all that, at least for the generation that immediately followed. People began to see their retirement plan as a government entitlement and one that they would earn through weekly or bi-weekly payroll deductions, throughout their working careers.

The first known employer-sponsored pension plan in America was established by the American Express Company in 1875, then a stagecoach delivery service[28]. It was by far the exception. Prior to the development of corporate pension plans, companies might move older workers to marginal employment at lower wages, or let them go altogether, as most workers held no vested rights to any form of pension plan[29]. In 1900, there were a total of just five companies in the United States offering their employees company-sponsored retirement plans.

The enactment of the Revenue Act of 1921, however, exempted the income of pension trusts from taxation, thereby modestly accelerating interest in the plans. Similarly, the Revenue Act of 1928 permitted employers' tax deductions for reasonable contributions into employee pension plans, adding further incentive for corporate support of retirement plans. Yet still by 1929, only 397 private sector retirement plans were in operation in the US and Canada. Their widespread use in Corporate America would not catch on for quite some time. And with pensions that were in practice often granted or withheld at the employer's option, by 1932, only about 5% of elderly workers would ever see any retirement pension at all[30].

At the same time, many changes were taking place in America, including the Industrial Revolution and more ominously, the trading in shares of many of these new companies. It was at this moment in time, on black Friday, October 24, 1929 that events conspired to bring about the epic crash of the stock market and its devastating impact on the global economy. In a period of just three months, forty percent of the value of the stock market was lost and with it, $26 billion dollars of investor wealth. In the following three years, by 1932, the Gross Domestic Product of the US would be cut *in half* and wages paid to American workers would fall from $50 billion to $30 billion[31]. The unemployment rate would soar to 36%.

Poverty rates among the elderly grew at an alarming pace throughout the Depression. Amidst limited retirement support from employers, the Great Depression raised a heightened concern for the care of elderly workers by the public. By 1934, less than half of America's elderly could remain self-supporting. The decade that followed saw significant growth in employer-sponsored plans. By 1940, following the greatest economic downturn in US history, over 4 million Americans were now covered by pension plans. Despite these gains, though, the number covered by retirement plans still represented only 15% of all private sector workers[32].

It was also during this time, and following many failed and desperate attempts at the state level, that the US Social Security System, which many today continue to see as the safety net of all safety nets, was put into law.

Social Security was loosely modelled on social insurance programs that had become popular in Europe in the nineteenth century. It succeeded many grass roots movements in the US to provide for the care of the elderly begun by Huey Long, Francis Townsend and Herbert Bigelow. By the time President Roosevelt signed the Social Security Act into law on August 14, 1935 at a ceremony at the White House, there were thirty-four nations that had adopted some form of retirement support or insurance for the care of the elderly.

The Townsend Plan, more formally known as the Old Age Revolving Pension Plan, is viewed as one of the most influential of these earlier pension plans, in terms of its impact on the development of Social Security. Responding to the devastating state of elderly care during the Great Depression, Senator Townsend presented a plan for the payment of a pension of $200 per month to each citizen over age sixty (roughly $1,750 in current dollars) with payments to be funded through a national sales tax on all commercial transactions. The plan would be open to all who were retired, free of a criminal past and with the additional stipulation that all monies received would be spent within thirty days of their receipt. Unlike Social Security to soon follow, the Townsend Plan would not tie payroll deductions to fund the system with the pensions provided. Rather, the tax supporting the program would be more broadly based, as a commercial sales tax.

The Townsend plan would soon become extremely popular in America, with over two million members of "Townsend Clubs" seeking to promote its adoption and with public opinion polls at the time indicating the support of 56% of Americans[33]. The program was ultimately flawed in its economic assumptions regarding revenue and expenditures, in part due to the monthly stipend of $200 as proposed, during a time when average monthly wages in the country were just $100. The plan was ultimately scrapped in favor of Social Security, to be initially drafted as the "Economic Security Bill", strongly supported by President Roosevelt and gaining favor in Congress.

Roosevelt had proposed the legislation in January of that same year, at a time when poverty rates for America's elderly exceeded 50%[34]. Introduced as H.R. 4120, the Bill was offered *"to alleviate the hazards of old age, unemployment, illness and dependency"*. H.R. 4120 was modified in committee and ultimately renamed as the Social Security Act of 1935 by Representative Frank Buck (D-CA). With the first participants paying into the system in the years immediately following its passage, workers would begin achieving eligibility almost immediately, with 53,000 beneficiaries in 1937 being paid a total of $1,278,000 under the Act.

The first payments were made in the form of a *single*, lump sum payment, and initially averaged just $58 (roughly $1,000 in current dollars). Try living off that for your retirement years! Through legislative amendment in the years that followed, however, the program evolved and by 1940 began its current process of providing monthly payments to beneficiaries. Also by 1940, just five years following the passage of the Social Security Act, an estimated 56% of men over the age of sixty-five entered retirement[35]. According to the archives of the Social Security Administration, one of the first to receive monthly Social Security benefits was a Ms. Ida May Fuller of Ludlow, Vermont. Her monthly benefit was in the amount of $22.54. Despite only having paid a total of twenty-four dollars in social security taxes into the system over the three year period of her employment under the Act, by the time Ms. Fuller passed away at the ripe old age of 100, she had collected a total of $22,882 in benefits from the Social Security Administration. And so began the precarious saga of the funding of the Social Security Trust.

And while Ida Fuller received the same level monthly payment of $22.54 for each of the ten years of her benefits, the 1950s would bring about yet further amendments to the Act, this time to adjust annual benefits for increases in the cost of living (or COLA). With rapid inflation for much of the 1970s and early 1980s, social security benefits climbed significantly throughout this period.

Perhaps the most significant changes to the social security program, however, would not occur until July 30, 1965, with the passage of the sweeping Medicare bill. In one short stroke of the pen, the Social Security Administration became responsible not only for providing elderly retirement funding, but also for providing medical care. Within its first three years of adoption, 20 million Americans would enroll in the Medicare program. And the liabilities of the system, as one might expect – at least one outside of Washington - grew exponentially.

And so, in a way, retirement funding has always been something of an *experiment*: an exercise in planning for unknown costs (or future living expenses) for an uncertain period of time (or unknown life expectancies). Perhaps Congress understood this when they enacted the Social Security Act. At the time President Roosevelt signed the Act, the system was designed to begin paying benefits to beneficiaries at age sixty-five, yet life expectancies in America were only fifty-eight. Hence, the expectation was that the vast majority of people would "expire" long before the funds on deposit in the Social Security Trust Fund!

But by 2008, the number of social security beneficiaries in America had grown to over 50 million with a total *annual* payout in excess of $615 billion. But with $927 billion in social security and other payroll taxes collected that year, so far so good. It wouldn't be long, though, before these two lines would ultimately cross. By 2013, the number of program beneficiaries would rise to 62 million, or nearly 20% of the population. The deficit of the Trust Fund in that year, or the amount by which the annual outflows exceed the inflows, would total $75 billion, a level at which these deficits are expected to continue through 2018, whereafter deficits are projected to *spike sharply upwards*[36].

At present, only one generation has seen the Social Security system function as it was designed to; that of Tom Brokaw's Greatest Generation. The successive generation, the Baby Boomers, now watches nervously from the sidelines waiting to see if the Social Security Trust Fund will be solvent throughout their golden years.

* * *

THREE

BOLT ON PROGRAMS FOR MEDICAL
CARE AND DISABILITY

What Roosevelt did for elderly retirement care under the Social Security Act in the 1930s, Lyndon Johnson endeavored to do for elderly medical care in the 1960s. Medicare was officially signed into law by President Johnson as part of the Social Security Amendments of 1965 in a White House ceremony attended by former President Harry Truman. In great deference to former President Truman, whom Johnson credited with the inspiration for the plan, President Johnson offered the following remarks, moments before presenting Truman with the first card issued under the Medicare program,

"Many men can make many proposals. Many men can draft many laws. But few have the piercing and humane eye, which can see beyond the words to the people that they touch. Few can see past the speeches and the political battles

to the doctor over there that is tending the infirm, and to the hospital that is

receiving those in anguish, or feel in their heart painful wrath at the injustice

which denies the miracle of healing to the old and to the poor. And fewer still

have the courage to stake reputation, and position, and the effort of a lifetime

upon such a cause when there are so few that share it."

Now that's great speechmaking! Medicare formed another pillar of Johnson's Great Society. In describing the intent of program, the President, addressing Harry Truman, continued,

"There are more than 18 million Americans over the age of 65. Most of

them have low incomes. Most of them are threatened by illness and medical

expenses that they cannot afford. And through this new law, Mr. President,

every citizen will be able, in his productive years when he is earning, to insure

himself against the ravages of illness in his old age. This insurance will help

pay for care in hospitals, in skilled nursing homes, or in the home. And under

a separate plan it will help meet the fees of the doctors."

The Medicare program arose in response to a growing national health care crisis, i.e., the great difficulty that those over the age of sixty-five were experiencing in their ability to gain access to private health care insurance. Prior to the adoption of Medicare, people over sixty-five not covered by an employer-sponsored health plan were at great risk, often left to rely upon savings or family to pay their medical bills. The prospect of America's senior citizens at the fringe of society unable to access basic medical care energized members of both parties to rally support for a broad program of government sponsored health care coverage. Through Medicare, medical coverage for the elderly would become a vested right. Like the Social Security program that it levered for its design and funding, Medicare would be financed through a separate payroll tax. These tax dollars, in theory, would support a self-sustaining fund for payment of Medicare expenditures.

From its beginning, Medicare operated in two parts. Part A would provide hospital insurance coverage at no charge to recipients, for those having contributed to the system through payroll deductions. Part B would provide optional medical insurance for which enrollees would pay a monthly charge or premium. The initial Part A deductible amounted to only forty dollars and the Part B monthly premium was only three dollars. Part A deductibles are now $1,184 and monthly Part B premiums run $105.

The program was greatly expanded in 2003 under the leadership of George W. Bush, who signed the Medicare Modernization Act to broaden the program to coverage of prescription medications. This added, optional benefit, would form Medicare Part D.

Within months following passage of the Social Security Amendments of 1965, more than 19 million seniors would enroll in Medicare. Today, nearly

50 million people are enrolled in Medicare and depend upon it for their medical care. This number is expected to *double* by 2030.

It wouldn't be long, however, before problems with fraud, inefficiency and fundamental economics began to emerge in the Medicare program. Today, no one really knows the full extent of Medicare fraud. In 2012, Attorney General Eric Holder reported on false billings in seven cities totaling $452 million. In 2010, a similar story unfolded of fraudulent claims by 94 people, including doctors, medical practitioners and health care companies in Miami, Baton Rouge, Brooklyn, Detroit and Houston, totaling $251 million. A Medicare Fraud Strike Force in 2007 found nearly five-hundred businesses in Miami that had billed Medicare for $237 million during the prior year - despite the fact that none of these businesses ever existed!

A recent report on Medicare fraud by the Inspector General of Health and Human Services found $5 billion in wrongful payments under the program in 2013. Including the six other programs that HHS manages for Medicaid, Foster Care and the like, the department *improperly* paid claims totaling *$78 billion – in one year.* Law suits seeking recoveries of suspected fraudulent billings are carried out continually by the department – *literally millions of such claims each year* (Medicare receives an estimated 1.2 billion claims in total claims each year[37]). The HHS report boasts a recovery of over $25 billion of improper Medicare payments since 1997, when the government first began tracking and actively pursuing these claims[38].

Perhaps the most interesting of these cases was a suit brought by the government of the Unites States against the City of New York in October 2014 accusing the City itself of defrauding Medicaid and receiving millions of dollars of improper payments via a computerized billing program[39]. The cost of all of this investigation has not been slight. With the Obama administration's war on Medicare and health care fraud, the tab is now expected to exceed $600 million per year while the recovery rate remains quite low. Roughly $4.3 billion was recovered in 2013 on an estimated amount of fraud and overcharging totaling $60 billion[40].

But taken in the context of a Medicare budget that pays in excess of one-half trillion dollars in benefits each year, these claims are important, but not altogether startling. After all, Medicare is part of one of our world's greatest bureaucracies with a total annual budget for HHS of just under *$1 trillion* and total employment of 76,000. The department manages 115 different health related programs, including Medicare. The largest by number of employees is the National Institutes of Health, followed by Indian Health Services and the Food and Drug Administration. Medicare and Medicaid, by number of employees, ranks just fifth[41].

The far broader issue for us here is the stunning growth of Medicare expenditures and, equally important, the projections for the immediate future. There were roughly 51 million Medicare beneficiaries in 2013, a number that is expected to climb to 71 million by 2024, as a growing number of aging Baby Boomers draw upon the system. While there are positive signs that certain reimbursable medical costs per person are moderating (due to factors that have largely stumped economists) Medicare like Social Security is on a crash course with insolvency, in this case by 2030, three years before Social Security.

The Congressional Budget Office estimates that annual expenditures for the combined major health care programs, including Medicare and Medicaid, are projected to rise by more than 85% over the next ten years[42].

* * *

DISABILITY INSURANCE

During the period 1965 to 2013, the population of the Unites States grew from 203,982,000 to 322,113,000, or by roughly 58%. The number of individuals in the US receiving disability benefits over this period, however, increased by 532%[43].

Started in the late 1950s as a means of support for those who did not yet qualify for Social Security, but had become too disabled to work, by 2012 the Social Security Administration had paid disability benefits in that year alone of just under $140 billion to 10.9 million people[44]. Today, the federal government is now spending more on disability than it does on food stamps and welfare combined[45]. Because most of these people do not work, they are not counted among the unemployed or as part of the labor force. Bear in mind, disability is defined by the federal government as a condition that makes it impossible to work.

Disability Insurance is part of the Old Age, Survivors and Disability Insurance program (or OASDI). Old age and survivors insurance is what we traditionally think of as Social Security. These are the monthly payments that the Social Security Administration provides to retirees and survivors of deceased workers. Disabled former workers receive monthly benefits under Disability Insurance (DI). The funds required to make both types of payments form the OASI and DI Trust funds, administered by the Social Security Administration under the US Department of Treasury, as established under the Social Security Act. Together with payments under Medicare, also administered by SSA, *these payments amounted to 41% of the total expenditures of the federal government in 2013.* In the 2014 summary of the programs prepared for the Social Security and Medicare Boards of Trustees, the SSA projects that both programs will continue to grow at rates *"substantially in excess"* of GDP through mid-2033[46].

Disability payments have roughly doubled in just the past ten years, alone. Like Medicare, some of these payments were in error, including 7,000 federal employees who received benefits in 2008 while also receiving federal paychecks or the 62,000 individuals who renewed driver's licenses after the SSA determined that they were eligible for full disability[47]. But the alarming rate of increase of disability payments in the years following the financial crisis has now become a cause of great concern.

In a report of the Richmond Federal Reserve Bank in 2012, the following sad facts on the state of the recovery from the 2008 financial crisis were delivered, *"As of July 2012, there were 811,000 more long-term unemployed in the US than when the recession officially ended in June 2009, and an additional 412,000 who had given up looking for work".* According to records of the Social Security Administration, while disability awards had risen at an average annual rate of 2% from 2003-2007, awards rose by 8.7% in 2008, 10% in 2009 and 6.8% in 2010. The author of the particular report questions whether those who have suddenly dropped out of the labor force, as reflected in declining labor participation rates, have been filing disability claims as a means of financial support, and whether these added claims have accelerated the demise of resources for the Social Security Disability Insurance program (SSDI)[48].

Nearly 1.5 million workers applied for disability benefits in the first half of 2012, more than all who applied in the full year 1998. In 2012, in total, accounting for those who have exited the program due to employment or eligibility for Social Security, there were 6.6 people on disability per 100 working, double the rate from twenty years prior and triple what it was in the mid-1970s. This rapid rise in disability has occurred despite the fact that the general health of people between the ages of fifty and sixty-five has greatly improved over this period of time. At the same time, the average age of those receiving disability benefits has *decreased* for both men and women, implying younger and younger applicants for disability each year.

Part of the reason for the rapid increase in disability claims can be attributed to the weak post-recovery employment market, but it may also be attributable to the broadened definition of what is considered disabled under the 1984 amendments to the program. These amendments in effect shifted the criteria in applying for program benefits in many cases from observable to *reported* conditions. The results are fairly stunning. In 1981, reported back pain accounted for only 17% of new cases, but by 2010 it represented 33% of cases. Similarly, mood disorders now account for 15% of all current disability claims. Some have found a distinct correlation with the exhaustion of unemployment benefits and the heightened incidence of disability claims[49].

Further accelerating the growth of disability, oddly, may have been welfare reform under the Clinton administration. Enacted into law in 1996, the Welfare Reform Act was designed to reduce the dependency on welfare (but perhaps not so much as it was designed to reduce the dependency upon the federal government). By transferring welfare funding to the states, the federal government sought to lessen its role in funding the welfare program. And with great latitude in administering the program, states were quick to comply - welfare rolls were cut by two-thirds in a matter of years[50]. The problem would soon become, however, a matter of trading one mechanism of public support for another. While states were burdened by funding welfare, their burdens shrank with disability, which continues to be funded by the federal government. And so we see, as with retirement funding, caring for those with disabilities appears to be yet another hot potato that our nation would prefer to pass around.

The rapid rise of disability benefits is also accelerating the drain on Medicare resources, due to a provision of Disability Insurance that provides for automatic coverage under Medicare after two years on disability. Amidst this rapid level of benefits increases, the reserves of the Disability Insurance portion of the Social Security Trust Fund have come under attack. It is now projected that the Disability Fund will no longer be able to pay full benefits beyond 2016 without Congress intervening to shore up the program's reserves. This projection lies amidst a policy proposal from Treasury Secretary Jack Lew to divert a greater share of FICA payroll tax from Social Security to disability.

Disability insurance pays about $13,000 per year, or just below that of a minimum wage job. For the *ten million* Americans who are currently on the program, they will unfortunately sacrifice not only income, but opportunity, as job skills tend to atrophy quickly. They will also sacrifice advancement. And unless they rely upon a spouse for support or quickly find their way back to work, the research shows they're likely locked into a cycle of poverty for some time to come.

Whatever the future of Medicare and Disability may be, one fact is becoming increasingly clear. For most retirees, even with access to Medicare, health care out of pocket costs still represent the largest expenses during retirement – and this excludes the cost of any nursing home or assisted living facility. Total out of pocket expenses for medical care in retirement for a couple retiring in 2014 are now estimated to total $220,000[51].

* * *

FOUR

A PEEK UNDER THE SOCIAL SECURITY TENT

For the typical household today, despite its level of payout falling well below median family wages, Social Security still provides the greatest share of retirement income. According to records of the Social Security Administration (SSA) 52% of married couples and 74% of unmarried people over age sixty-five receive more than half of their income from Social Security. Thirty-five percent rely on it almost exclusively. For lower income households, the share is much greater

One must also take into consideration the level of benefits of Social Security, relative to modern day costs of living. Average payments to beneficiaries are currently in the range of $1,300 per month and are taxable. This places the retiree who relies solely upon Social Security at a point below the poverty line. Further, changes to the "Full Retirement Age", the age at which workers are entitled to full benefits under the program, are moving full benefits from age

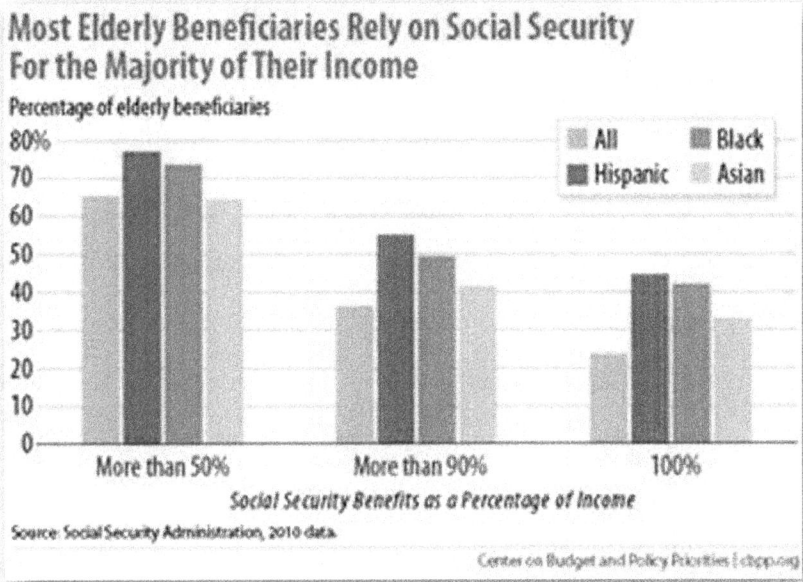

Most Elderly Beneficiaries Rely on Social Security For the Majority of Their Income

Percentage of elderly beneficiaries

[Figure: Bar chart showing percentage of elderly beneficiaries with legend: All, Black, Hispanic, Asian. Y-axis from 0 to 80%. X-axis categories: More than 50%, More than 90%, 100%. X-axis label: Social Security Benefits as a Percentage of Income]

Source: Social Security Administration, 2010 data.

Center on Budget and Policy Priorities | cbpp.org

Figure 4.1

65 to 67. Currently, only those individuals born prior to 1937 would qualify for full retirement at age 65. For those born after 1942, the full retirement age moves to 66 and for those born after 1959, that age moves to 67. For those who plan to continue to retire at 65, as many have in the past, these workers will see a reduced rate of benefits relative to that of full retirement age.

It's also important to consider that for the generation that preceded the Baby Boomers, the Greatest Generation as Tom Brokaw has dubbed them, Social Security was most often supplemented by employer sponsored pension plans. By 1980 the proportion of private sector workers covered by corporate sponsored defined benefit plans had climbed to 38%[52]. Public employee retirement systems covered an additional 8-10%. The combination of employer provided retirement benefits and Social Security payments thus provided, at least for many of this generation, a reasonably comfortable retirement.

Unfortunately, for the Baby Boomers who follow, the employer-sponsored retirement plan was largely phased out by the emergence of defined contribution or 401(k) plans adopted in the early 1980s. And so for the Baby Boomers, the largest generation of retirees in US history, many must look only to personal savings, either through 401(k)s, IRAs or other plans, to supplement the low levels of funding provided under the Social Security system. And then, of course, there is also the question about the future solvency of the Social Security Trust Fund, the reserves the Social Security Administration maintains against future liabilities to beneficiaries.

The problem originates with the fact that unlike the many pension systems that the Federal government regulates under ERISA, Social Security is run as a PAYGO (or pay-as-you-go) system. In years where inflows to the Trust through payroll deductions exceed outflows to retirees in the form of benefits, the Trust records a surplus adding to the reserves of the Trust. In years where outflows exceed inflows - as the Trust has experienced in each of the past several years and will for many years to come - the Trust draws down its reserves. At the point where future outflows are no longer expected to exceed reserves plus projected inflows, the Trust becomes insolvent. Interestingly enough, the surpluses in the good years (where inflows exceed outflows) aren't even held in cash, with the excess cash "borrowed" by the government to fund other, non-related programs. Substituted for the cash is a special class of federal government Treasury securities, or IOUs. We'll return to this topic again later in this chapter.

* * *

The Social Security system today, following several amendments to the Act, continues to derive the basis of its revenue or support from payroll taxes, or Federal Insurance Contributions Act (FICA) taxes paid by employers through weekly, biweekly or monthly salary deductions of employees. The total FICA tax is evenly split between the employer and the employee, with each paying a tax equal to 6.3% of earned wages for a total of 12.6% (as of 2014). The payments are directed to the Internal Revenue Service and then paid into the Social Security Trust Fund (also known as the Federal Old Age and Survivors Insurance Trust) where they are administered by the Department of Treasury. For tax year 2014, all taxable salary and wages of employees up to the maximum $117,000 were subject to the FICA tax. Total expenditures of the Social Security Trust Fund in 2013, inclusive of retirement, disability, health and Medicare benefits totaled $1.3 trillion, representing 8.4% of US GDP for the year[53].

The Social Security system is designed to have current employees pay in or generate revenue for the Fund through payroll deductions or FICA taxes, with these resources covering the Fund's annual expenses, or payments to beneficiaries. In effect, we're borrowing from Peter (the current worker) to pay Paul (the retiree). The system worked very well through the 1950s and for the next six decades, as ever growing pools of workers (who contributed at rising tax rates) supported a relatively modest level of benefits. According to records of the Social Security Administration, in 1940 roughly 35,000,000 workers paid into the system, with only 222,000 retiree beneficiaries, or a ratio of current employees to retirees of 159 to one.

But by 1950, this ratio had already fallen to sixteen to one[54]. In 1990, just three workers paid taxes into the system to support each retired beneficiary. And by 2031, this ratio is expected to decline again, to just over two workers paying into the system for each retiree. Stop and think about this for a minute. Each of your children will be paying, through FICA taxes, for one-half of the total Social Security benefits provided to a retiree by 2030. This is a function of the fact that over the next twenty years, the number of people eligible for Social Security will increase by 56%, while the number of people paying into the system through FICA taxes is projected to grow less than 14%[55]. Now, what's unknown, of course, is how long these retirees will live and therefore draw benefits from the system. What *is* known is that a smaller base of workers supporting a growing body of retirees, is simply not sustainable. ``Nor is it fair to burden future generations with the sins of the past.

Meanwhile, when Social Security was originally imposed, payroll taxes were just 2% of the first $3,000 of wages and salary, or a maximum of just $60 per year (roughly $1,050 in current dollars). By 1960, however, the tax rate had tripled, on its way to today's present level of 12.5% (with these amounts equally split between employer and employee). That puts the maximum worker contribution in 2015 at just under $7,500 (with an equal contribution by employers) or *seven times greater* than what the maximum worker contribution was when Social Security first went into effect (adjusted for inflation). It's now estimated that 82% of American households pay more in FICA payroll taxes than they do in federal income taxes[56], yet the OASDI, the Trust fund for Social Security and disability is underfunded by an estimated *$10.6 trillion*[57].

Increases in longevity are a critical factor contributing to greater projected shortfalls for the Social Security Trust Fund. At the time Social Security was fully implemented in 1940, life expectancies for men reaching the full retirement age of sixty-five were less than twelve years (interestingly, life expectancy for the cohort who turned 65 in 1940, or who were born in 1875 was significantly less than the retirement age). By 2013, however, the added life expectancy to be funded through Social Security had climbed to eighteen years, while the full retirement age was pushed back only one year, to age sixty-six. This change in life expectancy equates to a 43% increase in the length of retirement to be covered under Social Security benefits (and 45% for retiring women)[58].

The 1983 amendments were designed to address this forecasted imbalance as the pending retirement of the Baby Boomers began to come into view. Payroll taxes were raised. No sooner did the surpluses build, however, than claims of Congress raiding the Social Security Trust Fund began to emerge. Again, remember, these interim surpluses were planned and provided for in an effort to offset growing future liabilities of the Trust Fund. But the swapping of Treasury bonds for the cash surpluses became irresistible and an immediate source of political debate. This also means that you, the future retiree and social security recipient are in effect the holders of these IOUs. While the Treasury bonds represent an asset of the Trust Fund, they also represent an equal *liability* to the U.S. Treasury who must come up with revenue to pay them.

The Office of Management and Budget in 2000 characterized the circumstances of the Trust Fund, as follows *"these balances are available to finance future benefit payments…only in a bookkeeping sense. They do not consist of real economic assets that can be drawn down in the future to fund benefits. Instead, they are claims on the Treasury that, when redeemed, will have to be financed by raising taxes, borrowing from the public, or by reducing benefits or other expenditures"*[59].

* * *

In 2010, the Social Security system ran one of its first ever deficits of $49 billion, with monies withdrawn from the Trust Fund to cover the shortfall.

As previously mentioned, deficits are now running in the range of $75 billion per year and are projected to continue an upwards trajectory. Each of these deficits of the Social Security Trust Fund is being met by an additional and equal US Treasury obligation or bond. So while Treasury bonds were issued in surplus years to allow Congress to raid the cash *surpluses* of the Social Security Trust Fund, now in the lean years the Treasury is again relying upon the issuance of bonds to fund *deficits* in order to avoid directly funding the shortfalls with cash. It's little wonder then that the largest holder of US Treasury bonds isn't China or Japan, or even the Federal Reserve Bank. It's the Social Security Trust Fund.

Social Security now holds roughly 16% of the $18 trillion of the nation's debt, or approximately $2.8 trillion. The problem with this approach is that Treasury bonds are simply promises to pay cash from future resources. Since the vast majority of the government's resources are taxes, principally individual income and payroll taxes, that means you and I will need to help the government make good on its promises to pay Social Security. But that tax burden, few may realize, is without restoring Social Security's *solvency*. Rather, additional tax revenues will be necessary just to pay the US Treasury bonds already held by the Trust, without impacting the Trust Fund's current projected date of insolvency.

A 2013 report of the Social Security Administration (the "SSA") indicated that the Social Security Trust Fund on its current trajectory would run out of reserves by 2033[60]. The prevailing argument of the SSA in the report is that either Congress would need to "intervene" to address this imbalance, or the SSA would be forced to cut retiree benefits. By intervention, the SSA is implying that Congress would need to approve tax increases or the redirection of other existing budget resources in order to provide for the benefits of the Social Security Trust Fund. The disability trust fund, once again, that comprises part of this same OASDI Trust Fund is due to deplete by *2016* (according to the SSA report, the disability program spent $132 billion on beneficiary payments in 2011, while taking in just $106 billion). Upon depletion, the SSA estimates that it will be able to meet just 77% of scheduled benefits.

It's worth pointing out that the estimates of future insolvency of the Social Security Administration are subject to annual revision. The 1983 report of the SSA, for instance, projected a future date of insolvency of 2058. These estimates have been continually revised throughout the years, with a decided trend towards earlier and earlier dates of insolvency. In the past five years, the projected date of insolvency has come in by eight years to its current date of 2033. Research by the Heritage Foundation indicates that the date of insolvency of the Social Security Trust Fund could be much sooner than the SSA predicts, as much as nine years earlier, or 2024[61].

Recessions, such as that which the nation faced in 2008-2009 following the financial crisis, can have devastating impacts on the balances of the Social Security Trust Fund. Lower employment, declining wages and average hours worked, even lower birth rates all exert downward forces on the revenue to support the fund, while higher claims for disability raise the Fund's payouts.

Plans for solving the Social Security crisis have already been put forth by both Democrats and Republicans, becoming part of the clamor of the 2008 and 2012 Presidential debates and likely many more to come. Some in Congress continue to argue against the findings of the Social Security Administration, doubting the accuracy of their projections, or relying upon the expected twenty-years of remaining solvency as sufficient time to address the problem. Max Bacus (D-MT) Chairman of the Senate Finance Committee when presented with the SSA report argued just this, *"The program will be fully funded for more than twenty years, we have time to find smart ways to improve it"*, or at least someone does, long after Bacus has retired from Congress (Senator Bacus left the Congress in 2014 and is presently United States Ambassador to China).

But one point upon which most agree is that a weak economy further endangers the solvency of the program, as greater levels of unemployment impair payroll deductions. Oddly, lower interest rates, engineered to stimulate other areas of the economy, also work to the detriment of the Trust Fund as some $2.7 trillion of the Trust Fund's assets are held in US Treasury securities. While the average interest rate on Trust Fund balances in the early 1990s was running as high as 9%, the average interest rate on the Fund for 2013 was only 3.47%[62]. Lower interest rates may reduce borrowing costs for the US Treasury (and, therefore, greatly lower the federal budget deficit) but low interest rates also generate lower investment *income* for the Trust Fund.

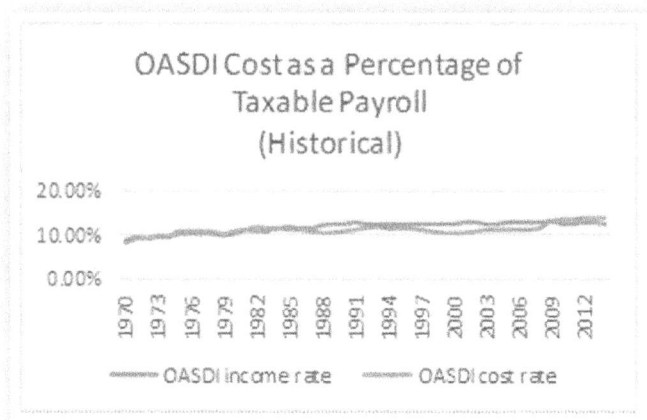

Figure 4.2
Source: Social Security Administration

While the Fund has been growing in most years and totaled $2.7 trillion in 2013, the rate of investment income will now be slowing significantly at the same time that beneficiary payments to retiring Baby Boomers (and also life expectancies) will be rising. Many now believe these critical factors have been significantly underestimated by the Social Security Administration – to the tune of $800 billion by 2013[63]. While this would only shorten the solvency of the Fund by an additional two years from the Administration's forecast, or to 2031, the impacts of future economic growth on unemployment and the rate of investment of the Fund, two critical factors in generating reserves, remain unknown.

The future costs of Social Security were outlined in the Annual Social Security and Medicare Trust Fund Reports, submitted by Treasury Secretary Jack Lew and other Trustees of the Trust Fund (OASDI) to Congress in 2014. In their report, the SSA looks to future income and costs of the Fund expressed as a percentage of taxable payroll, as the payroll tax provides the primary source of the Fund's income. The historical relationship between income and costs, as a percentage of payroll is provided in the table below. The percentages refer to the portion of employee wages that are taxed to support the OASDI program only, excluding taxes to support Medicare.

Expressed as a projected percentage of *future* payroll through 2033, however, the table shows considerable growth in payroll tax requirements.

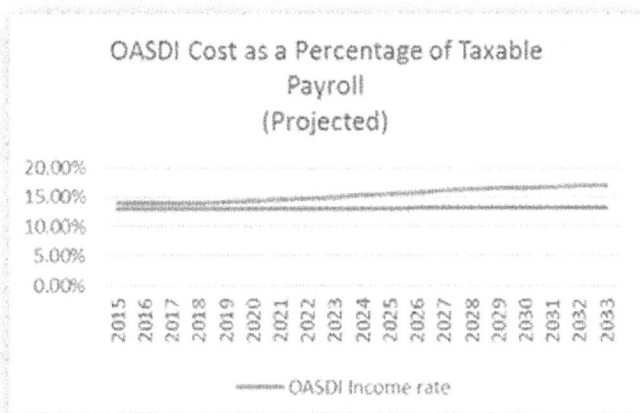

Figure 4.3
Source: Social Security Administration

While the OASDI income rate is scheduled to rise very slowly, from the 12.77% tax rate currently in effect to 13.18% by 2033, costs are expected to greatly outstrip the rate of income growth. Perhaps the most graphic visualization of the future solvency of the Trust can be shown by the following table of historical and projected OASDI assets relative to annual expenses.

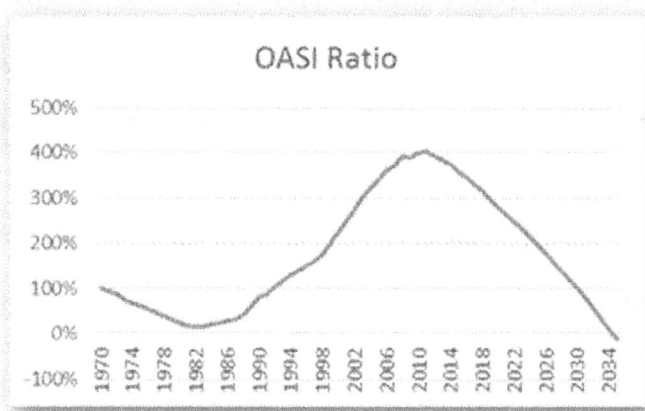

Figure 4.4
Source: Social Security Administration

Of course in making these projections the SSA takes into account a variety of economic variables, including mortality rates, productivity, consumer prices, real wages, the unemployment rate, etc. These variables are embodied in a report on long-range economic assumptions that accompanies the Annual Trustee Report. One of the most critical of these assumptions, in a system that attempts to match existing US Treasury security assets with future beneficiary liabilities, is the interest rate assumption that is modelled for the securities owned.

That interest rate on Treasury securities owned by the Trust Fund, as pointed out earlier in this chapter, has declined markedly over the past twenty-five years, from interest rates as high as 9% in the early 1990s to the present average level of 3.47%. While interest rates have declined steadily over this period, the zero interest rate policy of the Federal Reserve of the past six years has *greatly accelerated* this reduction in the average rate of investment. Many have speculated on the unintended implications of current Fed policy throughout the economy, but the lowered rate of return on assets of the OASDI is clearly one of the most unintended of outcomes. Moreover, as the special-class US Treasuries that are purchased by the OASDI from earlier years with higher interest rates begins to roll off, these securities are being replaced with newly issued, lower interest rate issues. Thus, the interest rate on the Trust Fund assets will *continue to decline* for several years into the future, even if interest rates *rise* at a reasonable pace over this time period.

As the SSA calculates returns based upon "real" or inflation-adjusted returns on US Treasuries that it holds, the compression of real interest rates over the past several years has also served to weaken the solvency of the Trust. After earning real (i.e., inflation adjusted) yields that averaged 6.27% from 1982-1992, the real rate of return had fallen to 4.10% from 1992-2002 and to 1.33% for the period 2002-2012. Surprisingly, despite this dramatic decline in the earning yield of the OASDI and the concern that the current economic recovery may continue to languish, the SSA currently predicts that interest rates will rise "modestly" over the near term as the economy and labor market continues to improve.

Projected interest earnings on the OASDI balances for 2014 are $99 billion, or roughly 3.5% on the balance of $2.78 trillion invested[64]. The interest rate assumptions in the report show further rises in interest rates over the years ahead, allowing the projected Trust Fund balance to continue to grow until 2020, whereafter, net redemptions due to an acceleration in retirees will lead to the Fund's insolvency by 2033. However, it must be pointed out that were the economy not to see strong growth and should interest rates not rise as strongly as projected by the SSA, the date of Trust Fund depletion could (and most likely will) be *substantially* earlier.

These shortcomings that threaten the future solvency of the OASDI can be addressed through an increase in the payroll tax or FICA rate, by reducing payout benefits to future retirees, by further delaying the full retirement age for benefit eligibility or by means testing benefit eligibility. But each of these measures presents its own set of problems. Raising the retirement age could accelerate poverty among the elderly population, as many struggle throughout their sixties and seventies to reach a full retirement age of 78, or 80 as has been proposed. Trimming benefits seems equally as unlikely, given that current benefits for those who rely upon them solely, place these people below the poverty line. Raising the tax rate could be recessionary or at least slow overall economic activity, as we recall from our recent experience in 2011-2012 when *cutting* the payroll tax rate was used as a tool to provide stimulus to the economy.

That leaves mean testing benefits, and raising the limit on wages subject to the payroll tax from its current cap of $117,000, as the most likely near term fixes. We'll return to this subject in Chapter 13. Regardless of what is ultimately implemented by Congress to restore the future solvency of the system, one thing is fairly certain and that is, no one is talking about raising the level of benefits. If you're counting on Social Security benefits for your financial support in retirement, then you better have another source of income be it employment, a defined benefit pension plan, ample savings or a sizeable 401(k). Either that, or learn to live on less than $15,000 per year in income.

In Chapter Twelve we'll learn just how big that 401(k) needs to be.

* * *

FIVE

EMPLOYER SPONSORED PENSION PLANS

O nce the leading source of retirement funding and the sole source of private employer-sponsored plans, defined benefit pension plans provide employees with established fixed future benefits, in some cases adjusted for upwardly revised costs of living. The plan's sponsor, the employer, bears the risk of investing its pension assets to meet these future benefit payments, much in the same way as the Social Security Trust Fund attempts to manage its future liabilities to beneficiaries. Unlike Social Security, however, employer sponsored defined benefit plans cannot be structured on a pay-as-you-go basis, but rather must comply with actuarial accounting mandated under ERISA. The employer plan typically retains actuaries and professional money managers to help manage these risks.

At one time, all the large automobile manufactures, railroads and much of industrial America ran their own defined benefit retirement plans. Some companies continue to do so today, although many like GM, United Airlines and TWA have sought to discharge these retirement liabilities through the bankruptcy process.

Defined benefit employer plans began to see a swift and prolonged decline in America, however, following the adoption of 401(k)/IRA legislation by Congress in the late 1970s. Today, younger employees are far less likely to be covered by an employer defined benefit plan than those nearing or currently in retirement. Traditionally offered to employees as a benefit in the recruiting process, employer liability plans represented 62% of employer sponsored plans as recently as 1983. But by 2013, just thirty years later, employer defined benefit plans comprised only 17% of offered plans[65]. According to the Employment Benefit Research Institute, today, only 3% of all US private sector workers receive their principal retirement benefits in the form of a defined benefit plan (reflecting the large segment of the private sector providing no plan offerings) with an additional 11% covered by a hybrid of defined benefit and 401(k) plans[66].

At one time, 88% of US private-sector workers with pension coverage received their benefits in the form of a defined benefit pension plan[67]. Today, of private sector workers, those covered by defined benefit plans are roughly one in five. For persons aged sixty and over in America, 42% report coverage by a defined benefit pension plan of theirs or their spouse's. This would include those previous employed in both public and private sector jobs.

However, as many younger employees were effectively "migrated" to defined contribution or 401(k) plans in the 1980s and 1990s, this number will be dropping rapidly. It is also important to note, that *roughly 44 million employees or 48% of the private sector workforce in 2011 worked for an employer that didn't sponsor a retirement plan of any type*[68]. These individuals typically work for small businesses and must contribute retirement savings to an IRA or SEP (Simplified Employee Pension Plan).

Defined benefit plans have also served the important role of minimizing the impact of gender and race considerations in rates of elderly poverty. In other words, for retirees with defined benefit plans there are less disparities among retirement incomes across race, class and gender. NIRS further concludes that controlling for factors like education, race, gender and employment history, those with defined benefit pensions fared better in old age than those without. NIRS refers to this phenomena as the *"pension factor"* – defined benefit plans exert an independent, positive effect on retiree wellbeing that, according to NIRS research, helped keep 4.7 million Americans out of poverty in 2010 (and with the government, thus spending $7.9 billion less on public assistance to elderly households).

This is readily understandable, when one considers that the mean annual pension benefit in the NIRS survey was $14,400. When added to social security benefits, this would provide a retiree with roughly $30,000 of annual income. Still below US median income, but well above the poverty line. Note also that while median defined benefit income for all former public and private sector workers was $14,400, this number varies widely between former private sector employees at $11,991 and public at $27,606, a subject that we will discuss in detail in Chapter Seven. Part of this disparity is explainable by the fact that many public sector employees are typically not eligible for social security benefits. Accordingly, their public sector retirement plans must reflect higher payments to compensate retirees for this fact. However, the NIRS research indicates that median *combined* 401(k) and social security income for former private sector workers, was still considerably below the median defined benefit for public sector workers.

Regardless of prior public or private sector employment, as we will see in future chapters, a retiree who was not a beneficiary of a company defined benefit plan and who sought to generate similar income through a 401(k) plan (i.e., the median of $14,400 per year) would need to accumulated a 401(k) balance or roughly $350,000 - or just under six times the amount of the median 401(k) balance currently held by pre-retirees.

We also know that pension income becomes vital to independent economic support in retirement. Retirees were *nine times* as likely to be living below the poverty line without defined benefit retirement plans versus those that are beneficiaries of such plans. Lest we think this is only a personal problem for these retirees, rates of public assistance are also *four times* greater for those without defined benefit retirement plans versus those that are beneficiaries of such plans. Not surprisingly, defined benefit plans also significantly insulated retirees from the dramatic effects of the financial crisis of 2008.

So we know the vital role that defined benefit plans have played in providing economic independence for America's retirees. We also know that these plans have served to keep more families out of poverty and off public assistance, food stamps and other government subsidies. So one must ask the question, with all this societal benefit why have we seen such a dramatic decline in employer-sponsored defined benefit plans over the past thirty years?

For the answer, we need to consider the impact of defined benefit plans on corporate balance sheets.

*   *   *

For years, General Motors offered rich retirement and health care benefits to its workers under concessions provided to the United Auto Workers Union. GM was actually the first of Detroit's big three auto companies to establish a pension plan back in 1950 as part of the "Treaty of Detroit", a contract with the powerful Walter Reuther, head of the UAW. In the years following World War II, high corporate tax rates increased the value of the deduction for contributions to qualified pension plans. At the same time, wage freezes during the war left pension benefits as a limited opportunity for worker gains, as their unions sought to represent them before management. By the mid-1990s, though, GM's US retirement plan had grown to 493,000 retirees and to the point where there were 4.6 retired workers for each active GM employee. It was estimated that roughly $4,000 of the price of a new car sold by GM went to pay retirement benefits for those employees already retired.

By 2003, the company issued $13 billion in bonds to shore up its struggling employee retirement plan. A great deal of money, but apparently it wasn't enough. In 2009 GM entered bankruptcy and together with the involvement of the federal government, engineered one of the largest government bailouts in US history. At the time, GM was the world's second largest car maker, having been recently overtaken by Toyota. Its 234,500 employees produced in excess of nine million cars per year in 34 different countries. In its bankruptcy filing the company listed $82.2 billion in assets against liabilities of $172 billion[69].

GM struggled with other issues leading up to its insolvency, no doubt, including too many models and brands. The company had also become somewhat out of touch with customer interests and demands, while facing aggressive competition from lower cost foreign manufacturers. While each of these issues contributed to GM's trip through bankruptcy, none weighed more heavily on the company than its legacy pension liabilities and contract agreements with the United Auto Workers Union.

By 2012, UAW wage concessions had driven average hourly wages of GM factory workers to $73 per hour, versus $44 per hour at Toyota and Honda operations in the US (both are non-unionized shops). Moreover, rather than laying off workers amidst a downturn in sales and production requirements, GM had agreed to place idled workers in "jobs banks", where they received 95% of their salaries and benefits while the company waited to reassign them[70]. Union rules also promoted internal operating inefficiencies in an effort to segment and protect various classes of jobs.

GM's pension obligation to retired workers in 2012 totaled $71 billion, or roughly $20 billion *greater* than the company's market value[71]. While the US government injected $50 billion of taxpayer money into the company in 2009 (ultimately losing $11.2 billion of it) bondholders of the company were largely wiped out[72]. Today, it appears that little else has changed about the underlying financial operations of the company, its continuing pension liabilities or its wage burdens.

Far smaller companies have also sought bankruptcy protection from crippling pension liabilities. Reed & Barton, a Massachusetts manufacturer of silverware and other luxury silver products recently announced its filing for Chapter 11, ending a 191-year history in the Commonwealth. The company highlighted its rising pension liabilities, possibly as high as $18 million, for pressuring the company into bankruptcy. The pensions of the 900 current and former employees of the company will be transferred to the Pension Benefit Guaranty Corporation. Chuck Daly, the company's Chief Financial

Officer said the pension liability became something "we could never get our arms around – it was a big cash drain."[73]

For as we will see over and over again, in varying sectors and contexts, retirement funding is a growing economic burden. If planning for this retirement lowers the burden on retirees, it must place this burden somewhere else. For this very simple reason, by the early 1980s corporations could begin to see the steam roller of greater human longevity influencing longer periods of retirement, and therefore longer periods of retirement benefits. Couple this demographic change with smaller future workforces supporting ever-growing retiree populations, the potential for lower interest rates in the future or greater volatility of investment returns for retirement plan assets, and you can quickly conjure up a fairly toxic brew for those companies continuing to offer defined benefit retirement planss.

* * *

SIX

CORPORATE AMERICA SMELLS A RAT

At the time of their bankruptcy filing in 2012, Eastman Kodak Company had a defined benefit plan liability to employees of $5.5 billion. Ironically, one of America's first major companies to establish an employee retirement plan, Kodak, through the bankruptcy process transferred its liability to some 63,000 employees to the federal Pension Benefit Guaranty Corporation, or the PBGC.

The PBGC, in theory, is sort of the pension guarantee agency of last resort. If a company fails in bankruptcy it typically seeks to have its defined benefit pension liabilities assumed by the PBGC. The PBGC is a US government agency, with its director appointed by the President and confirmed by the US Senate. The corporation derives its funding from retirement benefit insurance premiums payable by private companies who offer defined benefit retirement plans. Through this process, the Agency claims to (indirectly) guarantee the payment of private pension benefits of 26,000 companies covering 40 million American workers.

The PBGC was created by the Employee Retirement Income Security Act of 1974 (ERISA) the major employment legislation that sought to stabilize and insure retirement benefits promised by private companies. There was history of the federal government stepping in to pick up the retirement promises of private businesses, as it did in 1935 with the railroad retirement system following the Great Depression. More recently, following the 1963 bankruptcy of the Studebaker Corporation and the collapse of its pension plan, Congress initiated a ten-year effort in pension reform, culminating in ERISA.

ERISA immediately preceded another important, but far less noticed piece of legislation, the Revenue Act of 1978, the legislation that would ultimately create the 401(k) account. Paradoxically, given the legislation that quickly followed, part of ERISA's mission was to shore up the integrity of defined benefit pension plans and to insure the continuity of these benefits following a bankruptcy or major corporate business disruption. Paradoxically, that is, in the sense that the Revenue Act of 1978 would ultimately set the stage for a mass *exit* of defined benefit plans by Corporate America.

In 2012 PBGC paid benefits to a total of 887,000 retirees of 4,500 former company retirement plans whose liabilities were subsequently assumed by PBGC. That's 4,500 companies that formerly operated employee defined benefit retirement plans and ultimately transferred these liabilities to the PBGC through the bankruptcy process.

One of the largest of these cases of the past thirty years, is that of United Airlines. When United received permission from the federal bankruptcy court in 2005 to terminate its four employee pension plans, Judge Eugene Wedoff sided with United, who argued to the court that the airline could not emerge from the bankruptcy process with its retirement plans in place. The ruling released United from $3.2 billion in pension liability for three years to 134,000 current and former employees. Those liabilities were transferred to the PBGC (interestingly, United's total pension liability at the time was estimated by the PBGC at $9.8 billion[74]). United was soon followed into bankruptcy by Delphi Automotive, Delta and Northwest Airlines, with unfunded pension liabilities in the case of the latter two, estimated at $16 billion.

As part of United's bankruptcy reorganization plan, the company migrated its current employees to a 401(k) plan, a move that the airline unions had steadfastly opposed. It remains an open and unanswerable question whether the bankruptcy would have still been necessary had United converted its defined benefit plan to a 401(k) plan in the early 1980s, following the lead of many other major US companies at the time. Perhaps United would have filed anyway, and perhaps the fact that early movers to 401(k) plan conversions like Honeywell, Hughes Aircraft, PepsiCo and Johnson & Johnson have not similarly filed for bankruptcy protection, is simply coincidence. Or to be fair, it may simply be a function of industries with more favorable underlying economics.

Be that as it may, while many public companies have divested themselves of their defined benefit liability through the bankruptcy process, a great number of *healthy* US companies have similarly sought to limit exposure to defined benefit liabilities by freezing existing plans. While an outright conversion of an existing defined benefit plan to a 401(k) style plan is rare, and would face formidable legal challenge, companies have actively sought to freeze future benefit accruals to current or prospective employees by closing their plan to new entrants. Occasionally, these freezes have also encompassed the existing accrued pension benefits of existing employees, allowing those earned defined benefits to be paid out upon retirement, while future benefit liability would be funded through a 401(k) plan.

According to data compiled by the Center for Retirement Research (CRR) a total of seventeen large and healthy US companies froze their benefit plans in the period 2004 -2006. Included among this list were IBM, with 117,000 participants affected, Verizon Communications with 50,000, Sprint Nextel with 39,000 and Hewlett-Packard with 32,000 participants impacted. Each of these plan conversions were termed "partial" freezes, meaning the existing defined benefit plan was closed to both new employees and some existing employees (the exception was in the case of IBM, where the plan was closed to all new and existing employees). This list also excludes companies like GM and Northwest, then not in bankruptcy but facing considerable financial pressures, who also announced a freeze of their salaried pension plans. In its 2008 survey of defined benefit sponsoring employers, the Governmental Accounting Office found that *half* of these companies surveyed had partially or completely frozen their plans[75].

The act of otherwise healthy companies choosing to freeze their pension plans has accelerated in more recent years with Macy's, Allstate, News Corp, Lockheed Martin, Walt Disney, Boeing, Bank of America, Kraft and Clorox all joining a long list of household names seeking to limit defined benefit plan exposure.

So why are so many companies seeking to limit their defined benefit liabilities to employees through bankruptcy or by freezing their existing plan? The answers are, at least in part, somewhat obvious. In an increasingly competitive business environment, many companies are seeking to limit their overall compensation expense. CRR found in its study that reducing the employer contribution to defined benefit plans, on average, reduced pension costs from 7-8% of payroll to a far more modest 3%, under a 401(k) employer match. Since these plan freezes were not met with salary increases to offset the reduced benefits, total compensation expenses were lowered. This shift in retirement liability, according to CRR, was far more likely to hurt mid-career employees than new hires, many of whom tended to prefer the portability of a

401(k) plan option. This would suggest very little impact of the freezes upon companies' ability to recruit and retain new hires.

Companies are also acutely aware of the changes in longevity and their impact on benefit payouts, as well as the increasing risk of managing those future liabilities through investments. The rapid declines in the stock market of 2000 and 2008 accelerated this concern for companies, who subsequently sought to "de-risk" their defined benefit pension plans.

But the Center for Retirement Research also found that a key goal in freezing plans was often an effort to restructure total compensation due to projected increases in health care costs. While this is especially true in those instances where companies would provide post-retirement health care benefits, the rapid growth in health care spending for even current employees has pressured the total compensation expenses of companies in recent years. On average, health care benefits had risen from 2.4% of total compensation in the 1970s to 8.4% by 2004.

Another important reason for the change was the introduction of governmental regulations, beginning with the Revenue Act of 1978 that ostensibly favored retirement tax breaks for individuals, but also favored corporations. Allowing employees to contribute to a 401(k) retirement plan with pre-tax dollars allowed companies to ease the burden of their own responsibility for retirement funding. With more and more businesses offering 401(k) plans, competitive pressures to provide defined benefit plans quickly evaporated.

Further, the Tax Equity and Fiscal Responsibility Act of 1974 and the Tax Reform Act of 1982, reduced the incentives for companies to maintain a defined benefit plan by adding new disclosure and reporting requirements, resulting in greater administrative cost following a period in the 1970s when corporate profits were undergoing significant pressure. At the same time, these acts increased the attractiveness of defined contribution plans. Following these developments in the 1980s, corporate sponsorships of defined benefit plans fell by nearly one-half, and new defined benefit plan formations were virtually non-existent.

In part, the growing urgency of companies to exit the defined benefit pension business also stemmed from the steep losses that pension funds suffered following the 2008 financial crisis. From a largely funded status for most large corporate plans prior to 2007, these plans had fallen below 70% funded status by 2012, with an estimated deficit of $689 billion[76].

The Wall Street Journal in 2013 reported of a $3 billion non-cash charge recorded by United Parcel Service tied to its pension plan in the final quarter of 2012. The charge emanated from a reduction in the rate at which its actuaries discount its future pension liabilities, due to the lower interest rate environment then prevailing. Within the same reporting period, Boeing, Ford and Goodyear all disclosed similar gaping pension charges. In the case of Boeing, a lowering of its discount rate of just 0.25% resulted in a charge of $3.1 billion in its future pension liabilities. The company reported a net pension deficit in 2012 of $19.7 billion[77].

The overall impact on private sector employee retirement benefit coverage is quite clear. As of 2011, only 10% of private sector businesses offered defined benefit plans covering 18% of US private sector workers, in contrast to some 78% of public sector workers covered by such plans[78].

As one might also suspect, the incidence of defined benefit plans correlates quite highly with employee representation by labor unions. Of those participating in a defined benefit plan in 2011, the same study found that nearly 70% of these employees were members in a labor union, while just 13% were non-union employees. Participation also varies greatly by industry, with over 80% of private utility company employees covered by defined benefit plans, while just 2% of those in the leisure and hospitality industries were covered by such plans.

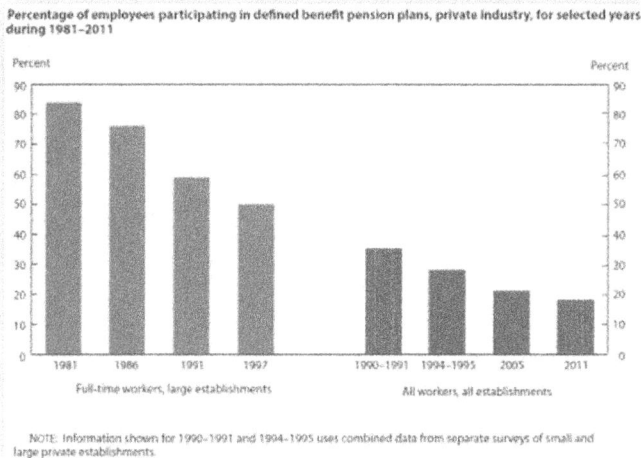

Percentage of employees participating in defined benefit pension plans, private industry, for selected years during 1981–2011

NOTE: Information shown for 1990–1991 and 1994–1995 uses combined data from separate surveys of small and large private establishments

Figure 6.1
Source: US Bureau of Labor Statistics

Bankruptcies and the freezing of defined benefit plans aside, pension liabilities continue to plague many American companies. The Labor Department estimates that 150 multi-employer pension funds, like the Indiana State Council of Carpenters Pension Plan and the International Brotherhood of Electrical Workers Pacific Coast Pension Fund, have entered "critical" status, defined as a funding ratio relative to future retirement liabilities, of less than 65%. While an additional eighty-five plans fall into the "endangered" category, meaning less than 80% funded[79].

* * *

SEVEN

ALL POLITICS ARE LOCAL

According to a recent article by Bloomberg News, the State of Illinois currently tops the list of US public pension funds with the greatest funding gap. This is something of an understatement. As of the end of the state's fiscal year 2014, the Illinois Public Employee Retirement System had assets on deposit in the system of just 39.3% of what is needed to cover projected pension obligations to current and former employees. The state's credit ratings remain among the weakest of all states in the nation, as those monitoring the credit-worthiness of the State of Illinois scratch their heads to figure out where in the world the state can possibly come up with the estimated *$167 billion* in funding needed to close the gap[80]. Yes, that's billion, with a "b".

Now, let's take a moment and put that number in perspective. In fiscal year 2012, the State of Illinois took in total revenue from all sources of just over $36 billion, or just 21% of its unfunded pension liability. If the State of

Illinois continued to take in revenue at this rate, and spent not one dime of it on salaries, programs or services – in effect, the business of running the state government – it would take the State of Illinois 4 ½ years just to pay off its unfunded pension liability, or the difference between employee pension benefit accrued liabilities (or, technically, the actuarial value of accrued liabilities) and the actuarial value of the state pension fund's assets available to meet that liability. In other words, it is an attempt to quantify the value of total future employee benefits that have accrued to date, relative to the projected value of assets and the income these assets will generate in the future.

This may leave the reader wondering where the money will come from for Illinois to actually fund what it is so committed to pay. It turns out the state's options for raising revenue are actually quite limited. Yes, there are a variety of sources of tax revenue, including taxes on gaming, utilities, motor vehicle fuel, beverages, etc., but the big enchilada is the personal income tax, accounting for over one-third of the state's budget, with sales taxes - also largely a tax on individuals - accounting for an additional 20%. In fiscal 2012, the state legislature in fact turned to its taxpayers, substantially raising the personal income tax rate (following a 30% rise in corporate income tax rates the year prior). With greater tax revenue, 2012 turned out to be a record year for the state's income, with revenue increasing by $5.8 billion. Despite the tax windfall, though, Illinois still recorded a budget *deficit*, as it has by the way in every year since 1999. It is from this platform of rising taxes and budget deficits, not unlike that of many other states, that Illinois faces the greatest challenge to its solvency yet - an unfunded pension liability that is *260%* of its annual revenue.

As if pension funding for public employees were not enough of a burden for the residents of the State of Illinois, their cost of retiree health care adds an estimated *$54 billion* of additional liability to the state's woes. According to the Illinois Policy Institute, the state spent $1 billion in retiree health care costs in 2013, more than double what it spent just ten years prior. Typically funded on a pay-as-you-go basis, these added liabilities are now growing at twice the rate of the state's tax revenues[81].

The alarms began to sound as early as 2012 about the pending insolvency of the State of Illinois. An op-ed piece in the Washington Post pointed to the problem and detailed the state's ill-fated attempts to address its budget imbalances through tax hikes[82]. Crain's Chicago Business reported as far back as 2010 of several civic groups and even gubernatorial contender, Andrew McKenna, as having raised the specter of the state's looming insolvency[83]. The most troubling part of all of this, however, is that few have heeded these warnings, *because truthfully no one – and I mean, no one - knows what can be done about it.*

The Public Employee Retirement System of Nevada for 2014 showed an unfunded pension liability of $40 billion. To address its unfunded liability, the state raised employer contribution rates – the percentage of total salaries that public agencies are required to pay each year to the retirement system - as a contribution to their retirement plan. In Nevada, the contribution rate for fire and police employees has skyrocketed from 28.5 % twelve years ago to 40% today[84] – this compares to just 8% for the average private sector employer sponsored defined benefit plan. Unfortunately for Nevada taxpayers, they effectively guarantee these benefits as they do with other general fund obligations of the state.

A 2013 report commissioned by the Nevada Public Employees Retirement System, just one year earlier, showed that the system would be fully funded by 2034. This projection, however, assumed that the pension system would earn a rate of return on investments of 8% per year for each of the next twenty years (a benchmark that the Nevada Policy Research Institute points out the system has only met *once* during the period 2003-2013).

The case of the Nevada Public Employees Retirement System, though, identifies another critical problem is assessing unfunded liabilities and pro-jected future pension benefits: the reluctance of the system to make its re-cords public. In the instance of the Nevada system (NPERS) records were ultimately revealed disclosing, among other findings, that in many instances annual pension benefits to public employee retirees were *greater* than their pre-retirement salaries[85]. But this information was made public only after a three year legal battle waged by the Reno Gazette-Journal who filed the request under the Nevada Public Records Act. NPERS resisted the disclosure, only to be ultimately required to do so by the Nevada State Supreme Court and then, only after appealing a similar decision by a Nevada District Court.

California is facing an unfunded pension liability of nearly $200 billion, albeit on a far larger tax base and population than Illinois or Nevada. Yet, the staggering pace of growth of this deficit, is a cause of great concern. California's unfunded public pension liability has increased *3,000%* over the past ten years, from $6.3 billion in 2003 to $198 billion by 2013[86]. Over the years, greater contributions by employees and public agency employers (i.e., by way of tax dollars) have been more than offset by increasing benefits and the growing number of retirees drawing benefits from the system. Interestingly, and deeply troubling, this has all taken place in an environment where total public sector employment in California has largely stagnated.

Pennsylvania is facing a $2 billion budget imbalance for the fiscal year 2015-2016. Its debt ratings have been cut three times in 2014 alone, placing the state two grades below the average state bond rating of Moody's Investors Service. The reason? The state's public employee pension system. State pension contributions are projected to rise to $3.1 billion by 2019, from $424 million in 2009. Last year, the state's contributions to its pension plans were only 52% of its required levels, a trend that is unfortunately, not unique to Pennsylvania. As a consequence, the state's borrowing costs to raise funds for a host of unrelated essential public expenditures, like roads, bridges and public buildings, will suffer as investors demand higher yields for the higher risk of Pennsylvania bonds. The Governor-elect's response? Raise taxes on natural gas production!

We need look no further than its neighboring state of New Jersey to see evidence of this dynamic at work. According to Bloomberg News, New Jersey, facing staggering unfunded public employee pension liabilities, saw *relative* borrowing costs (or credit-spreads) for a December 2014 debt offering that were "*five time greater than in its previous offering in 2013*"[87].

Separate from the woes of the State of Illinois, the City of Chicago, the state's largest and most vibrant city, faces its own challenges to its solvency, in large part due to grave difficulty in addressing its future pension liabilities. In a report by Moody's Investors' Service detailing a July 2013 downgrade of the city's bond ratings, Moody's cited unfunded liability as the number one factor contributing to the downgrade, "*[the city's] operating budgets are structurally imbalanced because they regularly underfund [future] pension obligations*"[88].

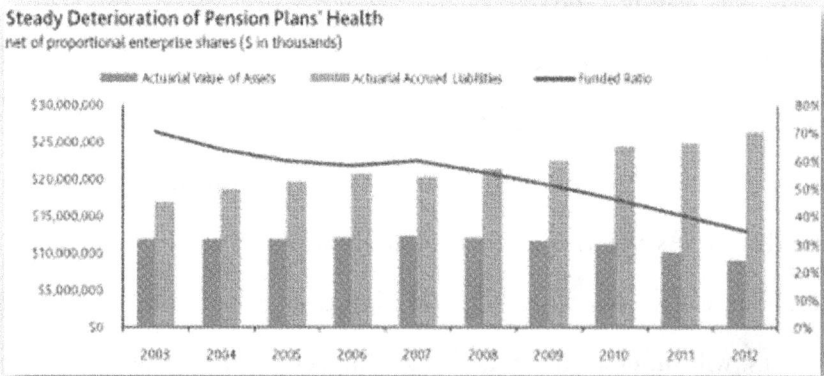

Figure 7.1

Source: Moody's Investors Service, City of Chicago audit

The downgrade follows a report of the retirement system actuaries pointing to an unfunded liability of $19 billion. The Moody's report continues, *"Unfunded pension liability growth will likely continue"*. A downgrade of the city's bond rating, among other concerns, prompts the increased cost of future borrowing due to the higher interest rates that investors demand of lower rated bond issuers. By failing to address its pension problems, the city in effect not only kicks the can down the road on funding its future retirement obligations, but also places yet a higher burden on its operating budget due to increased interest expense on future borrowing for non-pension related purposes.

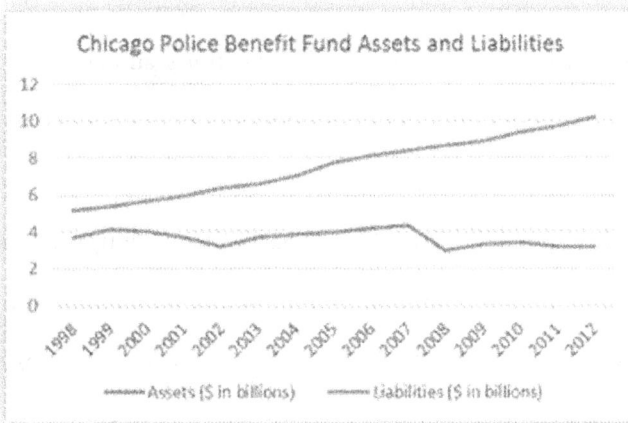

Figure 7.2

Source: Chicago Police Benefit Fund Actuarial Report 2012

The city's Police Benefit Fund reported a "funded ratio" or relationship of assets to liabilities of *31.4%* at the end of fiscal year 2012, or roughly $3.2

billion in assets against a $10.2 billion pension liability. The plan's unfunded liability, or the difference between the actuarial value of assets and accrued liabilities was therefore $7.3 billion, or more than twice the value of its assets under the plan. The fund's "actuarially determined contribution" for 2013, or the required funding necessary to keep the plan current based upon accrued benefits totaled $728 million, including $557 million of *interest* on its massive unfunded liability[89].

Most recently, Moody's Investors Service downgraded the public debt rating of the Chicago Board of Education, Chicago's public schools system to "Ba3", or junk bond status. Citing public employee pension pressures, Moody's placed a negative outlook on the school system's $6.2 billion of outstanding bonds (the Chicago Board of Education's annual pension funding requirements have jumped from $197 million in 2013 to $634 million in 2015[90]).

So what happened to turn these funds so horribly upside down? First, in the case of the Police Benefit Fund, average salaries grew by 55%, or roughly 4% per annum over the past fifteen years – not unreasonable. Average pension benefits, however, grew by 79% over this same period, while the number of former employees receiving retirement benefits increased by 45%.

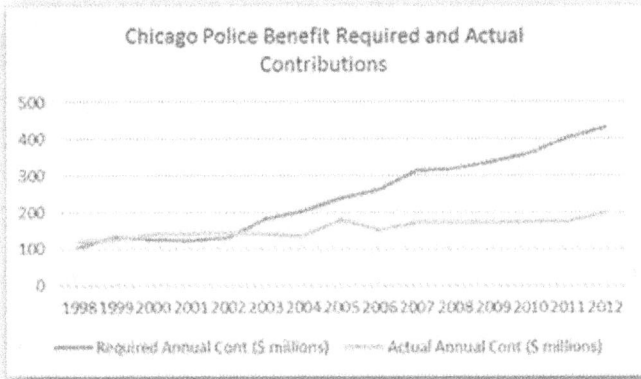

Figure 7.3

Source: Chicago Police Benefit Fund Actuarial Report 2012

Modest annual salary increases, coupled with rising benefits and an accelerated population of retirees, spelled soaring benefit payouts for the fund, with total retirement benefits growing by *160%* over the same period. Plan contributions failed to keep pace.

This same story has played out in countless cities in America over the past twenty years. As if these circumstances weren't dire enough, Moody's Investors Service points out that budget pressures driven by underfunded pensions will soon intensify, as the "*city's unwillingness to raise taxes and the state constitution's protection of pension benefits are formidable barriers to [containing] unfunded liabilities*"[91]. In other words, expect the pension problem to continue to spiral out of control. Recognizing these concerns and the failure of the city's leaders to address their pension underfunding, the bond rating agencies have been forced to lower the city's ratings, highlighting the added risk in buying bonds of the city.

In its rating downgrade of the City of Chicago in May 2015, also lowering the City's rating to junk bond status, Moody's cites, *"the city's highly elevated unfunded pension liabilities"* and continuing, *"we believe that the city's options for curbing growth in its own unfunded pension liabilities have narrowed considerably."* This thus points to the most troubling concern about public employee pension liabilities: that even well-intentioned efforts at pension reform will take years to slow the growth of unfunded liabilities.

For residents and taxpayers of the City of Chicago, the pension deficits of the city are additive to those of the State of Illinois. In a working paper of the Harvard Kennedy School of Government in 2012, the authors estimated that the household public employee pension burden of taxpayers in the City of Chicago – that is, each individual family's share of unfunded public employee pension liability - totaled $81,118, comprised of $41,966 for their share of City of Chicago liabilities and an additional $46,152 for the share of State of Illinois underfunding[92]. If you happen to live in the City of Chicago, you might want to start planning for how you will pay this obligation. Failing an economic miracle or a Federal bailout, the taxpayer is the only resource for paying this shortfall.

* * *

Of course, it's not just the state of Illinois or the City of Chicago that have suffered rating downgrades due to under-funded public employee retirement plans. Referring to the city of Philadelphia's pension as the "Blob" from the 1958 horror film, the city's Finance Director pointed out that the city now spends 16% of its general fund budget on pensions, an increase from 6% ten years ago. The fifth largest city in America, Philadelphia spent $648 million in fiscal year 2014 on pension funding, *$60 million more than it spent on its police force.* Despite these sizeable contributions, the city's employee retirement system remains only 47% funded, amongst the lowest of any major city in the US. Despite its recent contributions to the city's retirement systems, Philadelphia's public employee pension system is more than $40 billion underwater.

In his 2015 budget address, Lancaster, Pennsylvania City Mayor Rick Gray readily attributed his city's proposed 7.5% tax hike to state mandated increases in public employee pension funding. This increase follows an increase in property taxes of 8.3% in 2013. In his prepared budget remarks, Mayor Gray reported to the Lancaster City Council, "*If our pension obligations were the same in 2015 as they were when I first took office in 2006, I would be presenting you with a budget that cut property taxes by nearly 20 percent*"[93].

Its neighboring city of Scranton, in an effort to address its struggling finances and soaring pension costs approved a *50%* property tax increase in 2014, with a proposed increase of an additional *20%* in 2015. These increases follow a 2011 court order that, according to the Times-Tribune, awarded millions of dollars of added pension benefits to city firefighters and police officers[94].

The Auditor General of the Commonwealth of Pennsylvania, Eugene DePasquale, estimates that 573 municipal pension plans in Pennsylvania are either "distressed" or significantly underfunded. In total, his office estimated that Pennsylvania public employee pension plans are underfunded by some $6.7 billion. Commenting at the Greater Pittsburgh Chamber of Commerce meeting in June of 2014, DePasquale said, *"The crisis is that if we don't tackle this issue, we are going to have either massive tax increases, or we're going to have layoffs of our police and fire personnel"*[95].

Among state governments, Connecticut is right behind Illinois with the largest net pension liabilities as a percentage of total revenue of 213%, followed by the State of Kentucky at 180%. Measured in relation to its state residents, the State of Alaska leads with net pension liabilities of $21,352 per capita[96]. *This implies that the average family of four in Alaska owes more for their share of pension liability for state employee retirement, than they owe the bank for the mortgage on their home!* The liabilities are spread among a variety of public employee retirement systems. In the case of Alaska, the Public Employees' Retirement System Defined Benefit Plan, the Teachers' Retirement System, the Judicial Retirement System, the National Guard and Alaska Naval Militia Retirement System and the Elected Public Officials' Retirement Plan all contribute to the state's pension requirements.

Pension liabilities have now been cited as the reason for credit downgrades in Connecticut, New Jersey, Pennsylvania and Puerto Rico, as well as for the cities of Cincinnati, Philadelphia, Detroit, Chicago, Evanston, Omaha, Jacksonville, Des Moines and Minneapolis, among others. These credit downgrades stand apart from the local governments that have suddenly and dramatically plunged themselves into bankruptcy like the cities of Stockton, Detroit, San Bernardino, Vallejo, Harrisburg and Central Falls.

Part of the explanation lies in the law. While cities, individuals and private businesses can reorganize their liabilities in bankruptcy, no such provision exists for the states, at lease under current law. Without the legal ability to restructure their pension obligations in bankruptcy court, states faced with pension deficits similar to those of Illinois must opt for one of two unenviable choices. They can raise taxes, where possible to fund the replenishment of the pension fund, or they can reduce general services to residents to provide budget relief for funding the shortfall. But in many instances the tax route isn't just unpopular, it's simply not practical. According to Moody's, to fully fund the City of Chicago's annual required pension contribution *would necessitate raising its property taxes by 95%!*

At this point the reader may be thinking, well isn't there a third option? Can't states and other public agencies simply reduce retirement benefits? The short answer is no they can't, at least that's what the courts have ruled in case after case. This is precisely the decision that the Illinois State Supreme Court reached on July 3, 2014. In overturning a lower court ruling, the Supreme Court declared in a 6-1 decision that the "pension protection clause" of the Illinois State Constitution (and, as some have also argued, the "contract clause" of the Federal Constitution) states that retirement benefits are a contractual agreement that cannot be diminished or impaired. The Illinois court in its ruling found that this provision applies not only to basic retirement payments and obligations, but also to employee health care benefits if these were similarly promised.

In a similar case in the State of New Jersey in June of 2014, a state appeals court ruled that retired public workers also have "a contract right to cost-of-living increases". In California, the courts have ruled that *upon acceptance of public employment one acquires a vested right to a pension based on the system then in effect*. The ruling is widely believed to imply that from the day an employee begins work and begins accruing benefits, that employee has a right to continue to accrue benefits on terms at least as beneficial as that of day one, from that day forward. Further, if pension terms become more favorable in the future as offered by the employer, then he or she is also entitled to those *"richer"* benefits.

This vesting of public employee pension benefits has been taken to some extreme levels. Recently, the City Attorney for the City of Savannah, Georgia, advised members of the city council that they would continue to be required to make pension contributions on behalf of the former Savannah-Chatham County Chief of Police, Willie Lovett. Mr. Lovett, reportedly, had been convicted by a US District court for extortion and illegal gambling. He will be serving a seven and one-half year sentence in federal prison, during which he will continue to collect an annual pension of nearly $130,000. The City Attorney opined that Mr. Lovett continues to be entitled to the pension despite a state law that would require public employees to disgorge pension payments if convicted of a serious crime. The law, the City Attorney argues, was put on the books after the Police Chief was hired[97].

Several states, including Alaska, Arizona, Illinois and New York have state constitutions that specifically stipulate that public employee retirement benefits cannot be amended in any way that results in the beneficiary being paid a lower benefit, than as per the terms of the plan at the date of the employee's first eligibility in the plan. Thus, not only are accrued benefits protected, but prospective benefits as well. Michigan, Hawaii and Louisiana have provisions in their state constitutions that protect accrued benefits, but not future benefits that have not yet been earned. Several other states, including California, Massachusetts, Oregon and Vermont rely upon the contract clause of the state constitution to protect existing terms of benefits of employee, whether under contract or otherwise, as upheld by the courts as legislative intent[98].

Further, the political consequences of attempting to reform public employee retirement systems can be extraordinary. Take the case of the state of Wisconsin. In 2011, faced with a $3.5 billion budget deficit and soaring pension costs, Republican Governor Scott Walker submitted a budget bill designed to tackle structural imbalances that were undermining the stability of the state budget. Among these factors were expenditures for the state's public employee retirement system. The budget bill sought to limit collective bargaining for pensions and long-term health care costs. It additionally required greater employee participation in the funding of retirement expenses, raising contributions to 5.8% of salaries. The bill passed in 2011 and became law.

Almost immediately thereafter, recall elections were launched for six Republican senators who had supported Governor Walker' legislation, funded by the state public employee unions. Total campaign spending for the recall election, both pro and against totaled an estimated $40 million[99]. The amount contributed doubled the total spending on all of the state's 116 legislative races in 2010. While all but two of these recall efforts failed, the public employee unions have since turned to initiate a recall of Governor Walker, his Lieutenant Governor and four additional Republican senators.

The 2012 recall election of Governor Walker costing some $63 million was the most expensive campaign in Wisconsin's history, with the largest share of the funding coming from out of state sources[100]. Interestingly, it was the US Supreme Court's decision in regard to the Citizen's United case that invalidated Wisconsin's ban on independent expenditures by corporations and unions, including the National Education Association American Federation of State, County and Municipal Employees and the Service Employees International Union. Weighing in on the recall from their offices in Washington D.C. were the American Federation of Teachers, United Food and Commercial Workers, the Teamsters and the United Autoworkers.[101]. Despite the unprecedented funding for the recall campaign, Governor Walker, with 53% voter support easily defeated his challenger[102].

Despite these daunting challenges, both constitutionally and politically, many still believe that states and local governmental jurisdictions do have the right to alter retirement benefits for employees, although purely on a prospective basis for newly hired employees, where provided under the law. But this premise too has been challenged in the courts. Let's look at the case of the city of San Jose.

One of the richest cities in America according to US Census data, and home to such high flying companies as Cisco Systems, eBay, PayPal and Adobe Systems, the City of San Jose, in the words of the City's Mayor Chuck Reed is dead broke. In an effort to shore up its finances, the City cut its workforce by twenty-five percent, including a twenty percent reduction in its police force. Mayor Reed, a Democrat had defied union leaders and made pension reform a cornerstone of his administration. He was quick to point out the rapid and uncontrolled rise in the salaries of some of the city's public servants, including the police department, where the *average* salary in 2012 had reached in excess of $200,000 per year.

Retirement benefits for the city per Mr. Reed's report, amounted to $45,263 per employee each year. This followed changes to the city's retirement system that would allow police officers to retire at age fifty at up to 90% of their highest year's pay[103]. While total annual pension contributions for the city for retirement and retiree health benefits as recently as 2003 were just $72 million, by

2014 this number had climbed to $272 million, an increase in the annual rate of contributions of $200 million. Cumulatively, over this ten year period the city had increased its pension contributions by a total of $925 million. Terrified about the City's financial trajectory and staring at an unfunded liability of $245 million, Mayor Reed sought to take the matter to the voters. The unions sued.

On June 5, 2012, voters in San Jose as well as San Diego, California over-whelming approved ballot measures designed to reform their cities' public employment retirement plans. As mentioned above, San Jose's efforts at pen-sion reform, "Measure B", followed years of ever higher payments into its retirement system that saw annual contribution rise by 235% over a ten year period. Nearly 70% voted for the measure to modify retirement benefits by increasing employee contributions and establishing pension cost and benefit limitations for all newly hired employees. Measure B also allowed the city to temporarily suspend cost of living adjustments during fiscal emergencies, and required future voter approval of increases in pension benefits[104].

Promptly following its passage, however, the Public Employment Relations Board filed a series of injunctions against the voter-approved measure. To date these threats to San Jose pension reform remain unsuccessful. Even if these challenges fail, however, and pension reform is fully upheld in San Jose, the financial benefits to the city of Measure B - due to its impact only on prospec-tive, rather than current or retired employee benefits - will not be felt in city budgets for many years to come.

San Diego's Proposition B tried to move their city's pension reform in another direction, by transitioning future employees from a traditional public employee defined benefit plan to a defined contribution, or 401(k) style model. Despite its overwhelming support from the public and approval by more than two-thirds of voters, Prop B was again promptly challenged by the state's Public Employment Relations Board. An administrative law judge on behalf of PERB ordered the city to rescind Proposition B in February of 2013. Attorneys for the San Diego Municipal Employees Association claimed that the city violated its agreement to collective bargaining in bringing the measure before voters. Given the recent experience of these two cities, it remains highly likely that any future attempts of the electorate to reform public employee retirement benefits will be similarly met with legal challenges.

Detroit, in its restructuring plan filed with the bankruptcy court in February 2014, was the largest such bankruptcy filing by any municipality to date, in terms of the size of city and also the magnitude of the liabilities outstanding. The city cited in its filing $18 billion in total debt, including $5.7 billion in unfunded retiree health care obligations and $3.5 billion in unfunded pension costs[105]. While public employee unions are quick to point out that the average pension benefits are quite low, at around $20,000, benefits vary widely as they are tied to salary and the date of retirement. According to research provided by the American Enterprise Institute for an average Detroit city worker who retires after thirty-five years, benefits now equal roughly two-thirds of highest year compensation. With social security payments, total retirement income should average 95% of prior earnings. Far better than most Americans[106]. Further, while private sector employees typically fund the entirety of their retirements and, on average, state and local government employees contribute approximately six percent of pay, Detroit government employees paid nothing.

The City of Vallejo, a community of 115,000 residents off Interstate 80 in Solano County, California, was among the first cities in the nation to file for reorganization under Section 9 of the US Bankruptcy Code. Residents, businesses and investors alike were stunned. Now two years after emerging from a lengthy and highly costly bankruptcy process, Moody's Investors Service recently warned that the city may have to file for bankruptcy a second time. The culprit, as in the past, Moody's cites as pension costs, to total $14 million in 2014, up 40% from two years ago.

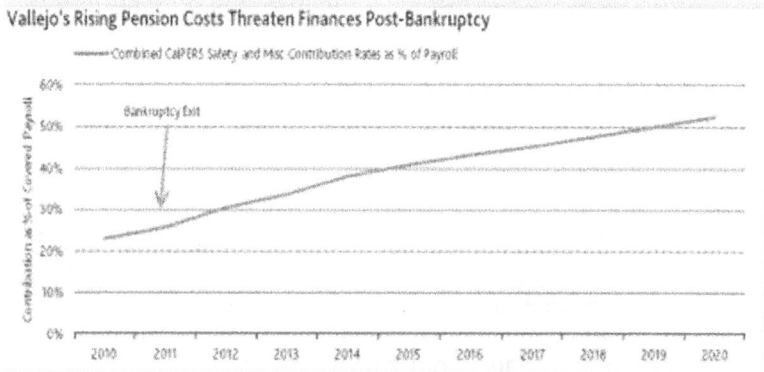

Figure 7.4
Source: Moody's Investors Service

Little was done in Vallejo's last trip through bankruptcy to resolve its pension costs. The pain, came at the expense of third-party creditors. Today, for those Vallejo public safety workers who have retired in the past five years average annual pensions are over $101,000, while city total pension expenses are projected to rise by up to 42% over the next five years[107]. Meanwhile, despite a one percent rise in the city sales tax to fund essential services, the city's streets are filled with potholes and three of its nine fire stations are closed. With employment in its police force down 40%, crime continues to surge, with homicides nearly doubling since 2006 and rising rates of burglaries.

Not far from Vallejo in the agriculturally rich San Joaquin Valley lies the City of Stockton, a community of 300,000 residents. After experiencing rapid housing development for much of the early 2000s, Stockton rapidly became ground zero for the 2007 subprime mortgage crisis, seeing its residential housing prices plunge by 39%. By 2008, the city reported the highest foreclosure rate in the nation. Faced with a steep decline in tax revenue, significant levels of debt and massive unfunded public employee pension liabilities, Stockton filed for protection under Chapter 9 of the Federal Bankruptcy Laws in June of 2012. In a recent and ground-breaking decision in respect of the case, Judge Christopher Klein of the US Bankruptcy Court ruled that public employee pension benefits *can be reduced* through the bankruptcy process, in the same manner as other debts of the city. CalPERS, the administrator of the city's retirement system had up to this point successfully argued in similar bankruptcy cases that under state law, public worker pensions could not be legally altered. In the Stockton matter, Judge Klein in essence ruled that Federal bankruptcy law trumps state law as to the matter of what can and what cannot be altered via the bankruptcy process. The Judge further denied legal standing to CalPERS in the bankruptcy proceedings, writing:

> *"It is doubtful that CalPERS even has standing to defend the city pensions from modification, CalPERS has bullied its way about in this case with an iron fist insisting that it and the municipal pensions it services are inviolable." "The bully may have an iron fist, but it also turns out to have a glass jaw."*[108]

The "glass jaw" reference in Judge Klein's comments refers to a lien on assets of the participating city, that CalPERS claims to hold, and threatens to bring to bear upon any city that speaks of exiting the retirement plan. Judge Klein ruled that this lien in not enforceable in bankruptcy court, a blow to CalPERS. Another way in which CalPERS "bullied" the City of Stockton, to use Judge Klein's words, is the process by which it calculates a termination payment should a member city desire to exit the CalPERS program. That process, to which Judge Klein refers, results in placing the city's retirement plan in a separate pool with a much lower investment yield of 3% versus the 7.5% of the general program. Lowering the projected rate of return on assets has the effect of magnifying the estimated future unfunded liability, in the case of Stockton, by $1.6 billion, a practice Judge Klein referred to as a "poison pill"[109].

The Stockton bankruptcy reorganization plan was confirmed by the U S Bankruptcy Court on October 30, 2014. While ultimately deciding not to reduce or limit public employee pension benefits, Judge Christopher Klein did rule that the CalPERS pension relationship is contractual and, therefore, *could be impaired* in the bankruptcy process. He did not require such impairment and, in fact, the City's bankruptcy reorganization plan did not recommend that this action be taken. The city, in the final analysis, *chose* not to challenge its CalPERS pension liabilities. While the confirmation of the plan represented a victory for CalPERS and former city employees, taxpayers and holders of the City's bonds didn't fare quite so well. The city sales tax was raised by ¾ % and bondholders of the City's $2 billion of bonds were paid in some instances as little as 12 cents on the dollar. The reorganization plan, while continuing to be contested by certain bondholders, went into effect in mid-February 2015.

As part of the bankruptcy plan, future lifetime medical benefits as promised to retirees were eliminated and replaced by an upfront cash payment, for which the former employee could purchase medical insurance of his own. In a press release in connection with the city's final exit from bankruptcy in February 2015 Kurt Wilson, the City Manager of Stockton, praised the city's efforts to expedite the payment to retirees, which must have felt like a bit of salt in the wound for the Franklin Templeton Fund, who lent the city $36 million in 2009 for various city public projects and will ultimately be repaid just $4 million. Wilson claimed that checks were mailed to the 1,100 retirees to compensate them for their lost medical benefits, saying, *"We made those a priority over everything else. They are ahead of everybody else."*[110]

* * *

The City of San Bernardino, California, a slightly smaller city of 205,000 located sixty-five miles east of Los Angeles declared bankruptcy in 2012, reporting a $45 million operating deficit. The case is proceeding behind that of Stockton. Subsequent to Judge Klein's ruling in that case that pension benefits could be challenged via the bankruptcy process, San Bernardino also *elected* not to tackle the CalPERS system. San Bernardino chose to restore all of its $24 million in annual payments to the pension system after initially withholding payments for months following its 2012 bankruptcy filing. San Bernardino, like Stockton, may get some relief by reneging on its promise to fully repay bond investors who lent the City considerable funds for rebuilding its infrastructure, but given the fundamental imbalance the City is facing in the management of its pension liabilities, this relief may, too, turn out to be fleeting.

The big enchilada of municipal bankruptcies currently lies unchallenged as to its size and scope. When the City of Detroit filed for bankruptcy in July of 2013, the city listed a whopping *$18 billion* in liabilities. After paying upwards of $135 million in legal and other bankruptcy related fees, the City of Detroit emerged from bankruptcy in November 2014. In its bankruptcy settlement, US Bankruptcy Judge Steven Rhodes approved the "elimination" of *$7 billion* of this debt, once again demonstrating the courts' willingness to punish investors for lending municipal governments money for their borrowing needs. But unlike the cases of Stockton and San Bernardino, where many of the governments' debt were backed simply by the cities' promise to pay, in Detroit, some investor holdings were wiped out despite the pledge of dedicated tax and fee revenues of the city. This precedent of unsecured (pensioners) over secured creditors (bondholders) was prior to the Detroit case, unprecedented in the world of municipal finance and, with the exception of the relatively recent handling of the GM bankruptcy, largely unprecedented in the private sector as well.

When Jefferson County, Alabama filed its bankruptcy petition on November 9, 2011, it called into question the repayment of $3.14 billion of its debts, then the largest municipal bankruptcy in US history. By the time its "debt-adjustment plan" was approved in November 2013, $1. 4 billion of its debt would be fully eliminated. The bankruptcy court, however, would retain authority over the county's $1.78 billion in continuing debt until paid off in 2048. The plan also required county residents to pay sewer rate increases of 7% per year for each of the following four years. Further, the courts, via an independent trustee and at bondholder requirement, could force increases in residential sewer rates at any point over this remaining period, as necessary to pay principal and interest on the bonds. The Jefferson County's woes were driven by corruption, rather than pension liabilities, with indeed four County commissions convicted of corruption related charges (as well as a $722 million settlement against a major Wall Street bank). However, the case highlights the risks of municipal bankruptcy assumed by bond holders and taxpayers alike.

*   *   *

The point of this discussion is not with the levels of public employee compensation overall, or how lavish promised pension benefits may or may not be, but rather to explore the costs of these future benefits to the local governments that are required to pay them. In this case, the cities of Detroit, San Bernardino, Stockton, the State of Illinois and many other local governmental entities, despite their best efforts to right their ship may inevitably be dragged under by the weight of their imbedded pension commitments.

In a recent report by Moody's Investors Service on the health and solvency of America's largest public employee pension systems, Moody's found that the unfunded liabilities of just these twenty-five public retirements systems tripled from 2004 – 2012 to just under *$2 trillion*. In a paper by Andrew G. Biggs, resident scholar of the American Enterprise Institute in July 2012, Mr. Biggs identifies the problem nationwide, using fair market valuation of public employee retirement system assets, and estimates total unfunded liabilities to total *$4.6 trillion*[111]. Moreover, this gaping hole in pension funding exists following a period where the annual pension plan contributions of US state and local governments have *more than doubled* over the prior ten years, from $40 billion to just under $100 billion.

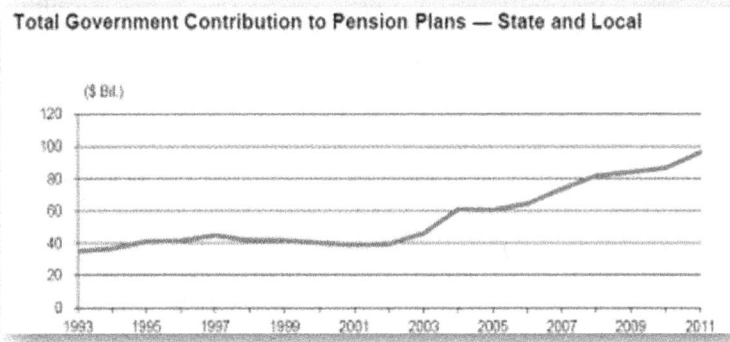

Total Government Contribution to Pension Plans — State and Local

Figure 7.5
Source: Fitch Ratings 2011

Moody's continues that the *"combination of aging plan demographics and the slow pay down of large unfunded liabilities effectively transfers costs incurred by a previous generation, [thereby] growing the burden on sponsoring governments".* In other words, the sins of the past – the underfunding of future pension liabilities – effectively multiplies, placing larger and larger burdens on the funding requirements of future generations.

Were this simply a problem like the mounting Federal debt (as if this were not an issue of equally grave concern) municipal unfunded pension liabilities could be rolled forward, potentially indefinitely. But the Federal Government has tools that are unique unto it, namely the ability to print new currency. States, cities and counties do not. For them, this is a problem of finite measurements and finite grace periods. At some point, required pension contributions will greatly diminish these public agencies' ability to provide basic services, at which point cities like Detroit (and *unlike* the State of Illinois) may increasingly seek out the bankruptcy process. *As to what happens to the states like Illinois, Connecticut, New Jersey, New York, California, and the others facing enormous unfunded pension liabilities without the Chapter 9 bankruptcy process available to them, it's truly anyone's guess.*

A case of just this importance is about to be heard by the Illinois Supreme Court. At question is the staggering unfunded pension liability of the State of Illinois, and a plan to modify some of its terms to help restore an element of solvency to the imperiled system. The state legislature passed a stopgap measure in 2014 to address the plan's imbedded 3% annual cost of living adjustment (COLA). The plan increases annual benefits to retirees of the system by this amount each year, irrespective of the actual underlying rate of inflation. With the consumer price index hovering in the range of 1-2% for much of the past ten years, plan benefits have nonetheless increased by the required 3% COLA. Lawmakers sought to reduce this rate, while boosting public agency contributions, all in a plan designed to bring the retirement system to 100% funding in *thirty years*, thereby saving taxpayers an estimated $100 billion.

The pension reform plan, however, was quickly challenged by labor unions arguing that amending the Illinois public employee retirement system violates the protections afforded it under the state constitution (similar to the argument made by CalPERS in the Stockton bankruptcy). But unlike the Stockton case where the US Bankruptcy court could and did determine that Federal bankruptcy law trumps local state law, the State of Illinois has no avenue under law to avail itself of the Federal bankruptcy laws. Article 9 limits bankruptcy reorganization to cities, and other local districts, but not the states.

Should the Illinois Supreme Court uphold the argument of the unions, and absent some economic miracle over the next several years, the state will invariably be required to dramatically raise taxes, reduce services, or default on its obligations – just not those to retirees.

* * *

EIGHT

CITIES DOUBLE DOWN

As of 2012, there were approximately twenty-four million active and retired public sector workers in America, constituting approximately eight percent of the population. Despite an approximate $2 -3 trillion in public pension fund assets[112], *unfunded* retirement liabilities for this eight percent of the US workforce are estimated at $4 trillion, or nearly $20,000 for each of the 203 million members of the US working age population.

Interestingly, this disaster has all somehow taken place in an environment of strong investment performance for public employee pension funds. Public sector retirement funds have experienced actual returns since 2004 approximating the rate of return assumptions that were modeled into many governmental pension forecasts (i.e., 7.65%). Disturbingly though, despite meeting their investment targets, the growth of *unfunded* liabilities has outstripped these returns by nearly 2.5 times, growing in excess of 17% per annum. To understand how this could be possible, let's backtrack a bit and explain the underlying economic model behind public employee pension funds in America.

Funding future retirement benefits to employees is first and foremost a matter of projecting what those liabilities will be. To accomplish this effort, cities and other municipal governments hire actuaries. The actuaries are tasked with projecting future payments out of the system based upon a population "census" or a modeling of current and future employees by age, life expectancy, marital status, estimated dates of retirement, future payroll increases and inflation. As many of these variables are by their very nature unknown, the actuaries access databases that provide statistical and historical evidence to support their assumptions.

Once the future liabilities of the system are modeled, the actuaries turn their attention to the assets that are on deposit in the system to pay these future costs. The difference between the two at any point in time, the present value of future liabilities and the market value of the assets on deposit in the plan, is referred to as the level of funding status. If the present value of accrued liabilities is $1 billion and the market value of assets is $800 million, the plan has unfunded liabilities of $200 million; meaning the current value of assets is $200 million less than the present value of future liabilities. Its funding status would therefore be 80% (or $800 million divided by $1 billion).

This fact, in and of itself may not be a problem, as it's the future value of the assets relative to the future value of liabilities payable to beneficiaries that will ultimately determine if the pension fund can meet its obligations. Thus, the assumption of the rate of investment return on that asset base and the growth in assets through new deposits to the fund, become critical variables in measuring the sufficiency of the fund.

To formulate this new calculation, the actuaries must make assumptions on the rate of investment the fund would realize over the remaining thirty or more years of the system. The average of these earnings assessments nationwide, according to Moody's Investor Service is 7.65%. This means that the average public employee retirement plan assumes an annual rate of return of 7.65% for the foreseeable future, or as far as pension liabilities extend. This earnings assumption is then used to discount the future liability to the present to determine the level of the plan's funding status. For example, if we assume a plan's future liability to be $1 billion, then using an 8% discount rate over twenty years would result in a present value of $210 million (or conversely, $210 million compounded at 8% per annum will result in $1 billion in twenty years).

To the extent the current market value of the plan's assets equal this number, the plan is said to be fully funded. Bear in mind of course, that an 8% rate of return involves assuming substantial risk. Thus, even 100% funded plans have imbedded market risk that could render a plan insolvent. Many experts would argue about the reasonableness of a 7.50% or 8% investment assumption going forward. Moody's, conservatively adjusts this return forecast to a more reasonable level (4.50% currently), while projecting total unfunded liabilities of $2 trillion for the twenty-five largest public pension funds, alone.

Hence, these 25 major city public pension funds are still beholding to a healthy and consistent level of investment performance for the foreseeable future (i.e., 4.5%) just to be underfunded by $2 trillion!

The following table illustrates the impact of the discount rate or implied earnings rate assumption on estimated unfunded public employee pension liabilities, based upon national state and local government data of the CBO in 2009. The sad fact is that it is not the pension plan or even the retiree benefits that bear the risk of the earnings assumption, but rather the taxpayer. Public employee retirement benefit payments are guaranteed by the local government under prevailing law, and 100% of the local government's revenues are derived from taxes. In the words of the Congressional Budget Office, government does not have the capacity to assume risk, it must transfer risk among its stakeholders: creditors, suppliers, employees and taxpayers[113].

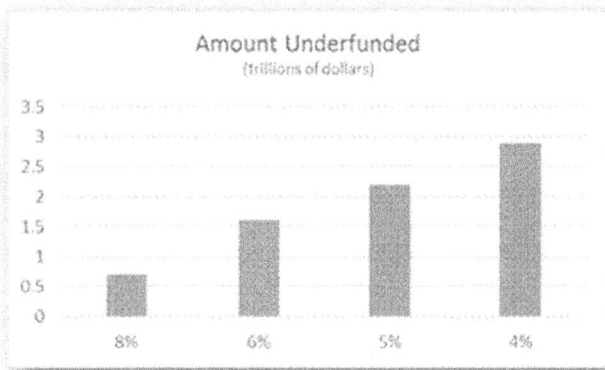

Figure 8.1
State and Local Gov't Unfunded Liabilities, Varying Discount Rates, 2009
Source: Congressional Budget Office Report, 2011

The growth in unfunded pension liabilities, as Moody's mentions in their report, is the result of inadequate annual pension contributions of the municipal governments, as well as *"the sheer growth of pension liabilities as benefit accruals accelerate with the passage of time, salary increases and added years of service"*. To understand how each of these factors comes into play requires some insight into the unique world of public pension accounting and the role of collective bargaining by public employee unions in negotiating the terms of these benefits agreements.

In California, public pension plans are often referred to as "three at fifty" or "two and one-half at fifty-five". What these numbers refer to are the percentage of highest year salary, in this case 2 ½ or 3%, and the age at which retirement can first be taken, or fifty or fifty-five. So for a city offering a plan of three at fifty, the plan would pay retirees three percent of the highest year salary beginning at age fifty. The percent of salary, however, gets multiplied by the number of years of service or employment. So for an employee with thirty years of service, earning $150,000 per year in their highest year of salary, the retiree could begin collecting pension payments as early as age fifty equal to $135,000 per year ($150,000 x .03 x 30 = $135,000)5. And these payments are required to be made throughout the retiree's remaining life (or to any surviving spouse). Moreover, benefits are adjusted annually for cost of living increases,

---

5 The California Public Employees' Pension Reform Act of 2013 (PERPA) limits maximum retirement benefits for newly hired employees to 2.7% at age 57 for safety employees and 2% at 62 for newly hired non-safety personnel.

throughout the term of the life of the beneficiary – another distinction from private sector retirement plans, where cost of living adjustments are extremely rare.

If this sounds like a ridiculously generous retirement benefit package for public sector employees, the reader may wonder where in the heck such an idea originated. "Three at fifty" found its way into the California pension landscape by way of Senate Bill 400, adopted by the California Legislature in 1999. Among other goodies, SB 400 provided the California Highway Patrol an increase in retirement benefits of up to 50%, by increasing their pension formula from "2% at age 50" to "3% at 50". The benefit increases were retroactive, not only for current or prospective employees, *but also for existing benefits that had accrued at the lower formula.*

The bill was sponsored by CalPERS, the mammoth California public employee retirement system that manages the pension assets of state, county and local governments throughout California. Local governments quickly attempted, and were in fact encouraged, to match the generous terms of these benefits offered to Highway Patrol, as a way to attract and retain public employees. The passage of SB 400, more than any single factor explains the astronomical rise in unfunded pension liabilities in California over the past ten years.

A Wall Street Journal op-ed called SB 400 *"the largest issuance of non-voter-approved debt in the state's history"*. CalPERS sold the program to the state legislature arguing that the increased benefits would not cause any rise in public employer pension contributions and would not cost taxpayers anything, while CalPERS would remain fully funded despite the greater pension liabilities. Sound too good to be true? It was. In its projections, among other items, the largest public pension fund in the nation also predicted that the Dow Jones Industrial Average would reach 25,000 by 2009 (the Dow Jones Industrial Average closed 2009 at 10,428). They also failed to disclose that CalPERS employees would similarly enjoy the greater pension benefits provided by SB 400, that members of CalPERS board had received contributions from public employee unions, and that the state budget would be on the hook if things didn't turn out quite as they predicted[114].

It's also worth pointing out that while these and other examples of public employee pension commitments might seem like they're based upon unique and unusually high annual salaries for public employees, according to the Los Angeles Times, there were a total of ninety-two officers of the Los Angeles Police Department in 2010 who earned in excess of $150,000 per year[115]. And we can assume they are worth every penny of it. The argument here is not with the level of compensation of these dedicated servicemen and women, nor with the reasonableness of their retirement plans. Los Angeles is a big city with great need for public safety and the work of these individuals is indispensable. But the cost of funding their retirement is nonetheless both an annual operating expense and a long-term liability of the city and, once again, the city's only resource in paying these obligations is its taxpayers. The City of Los Angeles is, of course, not alone in its growing obligations to current and former employees. The Peace Officers Research Association of California lists 251 public agencies in California with retirement plans of "3% at 50".

There are also the glaring excesses in compensation and in retirement benefits that catch the public eye. Bloomberg News reported in July of 2012 of the pension benefits being paid to the former Police Chief of the City of Stockton, a city which, as previously mentioned, subsequently entered bankruptcy under Chapter 9. The article describes how the Chief left the City at age 52 with an annual lifetime pension of $204,000[116], adjusted for inflation. Then there's the case of Bruce Malkenhorst, the retired administrator of the City of Vernon, California, a town of 112 residents per the 2010 US Census, whose pension benefits in 2012 amounted to $541,000[117].

There's also the case of Newport Beach, California a city world renowned for its beaches, surfing and Southern California lifestyle. Lifeguards there, as salaried employees of the city, are entitled to retirement benefits under the city's public employee retirement plan. The problem for Newport Beach taxpayers, however, is that of the fourteen full time lifeguards of the city, thirteen of them were paid more than $120,000 in 2011. Half the lifeguards were paid more than $150,000 and the two highest paid, earned $211,451 and $203,481[118].

After thirty years of service, at age fifty, these employees who were earning $150,000 in their highest year on the beach, will be entitled to retirement pay of $135,000 per year for them or their surviving spouse for life. For the lifeguard earning $211,451, after thirty years of service, this would amount to annual retirement income of $190,305 for life (its lifeguard employees, incidentally, are represented in collective bargaining by the Lifeguards Management Association). Despite such generous retirement benefits the city, it turns out, didn't quite have enough funds to actually pay for them. City records showed an unfunded pension liability for fiscal year 2011 of $169,157,000, or 243% of its payroll[119].

While these may seem like isolated and sensational cases, in 2012 there were a reported 14,763 retired California public employees receiving greater than $100,000 per year in pension benefits, up 700% in a decade[120]. By 2013, only one year later, this total stood at 40,000. Just under one hundred of these retirees received total retirement benefits in 2013 *that exceeded half a million dollars apiece*[121].

The State of Illinois, as of April 2014, listed two hundred Illinois public employee annual pensions greater than $196,000 and eleven-thousand retirees collecting more than $100,000 per year. Topping the list were ten former University of Illinois employees now being paid lifetime annual retirement compensation between $196,000 and $452,000. The estimated lifetime pension payouts to these individuals adjusted for age at retirement, ranged from $3.1 million to just over $9.0 million[122].

The State of Oregon currently lists 1,106 public employee retirees with pension benefits greater than $100,000. Topping the list was Mike Bellotti, former football coach for the University of Oregon earning annual pension benefits upon his retirement in 2011 at age sixty of $496,341[123]. Oregonians love their football and it's a good thing that they do. Assuming the venerable coach lives to his normal life expectancy of age 86 and inflation averages three percent, over the course of Mr. Bellotti's retirement Oregon taxpayers will be on the hook for retirement benefits totaling $20,000,000.

While not everyone has the talent to coach a top college football team, public records show that California City Managers in 2010, *on average,* drew salaries of $200,000 per year, while the top ten in terms of compensation ranged from $321,000 to $459,500[124]. Assuming 30 years of service, and using these figures as their highest base year of salary (and assuming a "3% at 50" plan) these employees would be due retirement system benefits ranging from $288,900 to $413,550 annually, plus cost of living adjustments.

Recent data in New York State shows that between 2009 and 2014, the number of teachers and school administrators receiving annual pensions greater than $100,000 nearly tripled, increasing from 1,600 in 2009 to 4,800 by 2014[125]. Recent estimates put the number at 8,000, with 90 retired New

York government workers eligible to collect annual pensions of greater than $200,000, four times the median household income in the state[126]. Moreover, in New York State, these benefits are exempt from state taxes. The Empire Center for Public Policy recently compiled a list of the top 100 New York State teacher pensions, with the *last* person on the list drawing an annual retirement of $164,472. Number one on the list was a former history professor from Queens College drawing a pension of $561,286. He was followed by a Brooklyn school principal whose retirement payments were $417,466[127].

In certain states, like Florida, a 1999 law forces cities to set minimum pension benefits for police and fire employees. Prior to 1999, Florida cities were free to bargain with local police and fire unions for pension benefits that fit the needs of both the city and its police and firefighters. The 1999 law, however, amends Florida Statutes 175 and 185 to require that certain city collected tax revenues be used exclusively for police and fire retirement benefits. The Florida League of Cities supports legislation to protect the powers of Florida municipalities to establish public employee benefit levels, including comprehensive pension reform and a means for Florida cities to extract themselves from the Florida Retirement System. Its research indicates that since the adoption of the 1999 amendments, Florida cities have been *forced* to devote more than $520 million of taxes to new, supplemental police and fire employee retirement benefits[128].

Then, there are also the all-too-frequent instances of municipal employees specifically boosting or "spiking" pay in the latter part of their career, through overtime or other means in order to raise their base level of compensation against which all future pension benefits are calculated. According to the Los Angeles Times who compiled a list of nearly 200 Los Angeles County public employees who earned more than a quarter of a million dollars in 2009, the Times found that only 65 people on the list made it there on base salary alone. The rest did so on overtime pay. One employee, a pilot for the Los Angeles County Fire Department earned $153,324 in overtime on top of a base salary of $140,504, for total compensation of $293,829[129] in his year prior to retirement.

The practice of permitting employees to add unused sick time, vacation time overtime pay and even mobile phone allowances as a compensation basis of pension benefits is estimated to cost the City of Phoenix Employee Retirement System as much as $12 million per year, when calculating annual pension requirements on true base salary, rather than adjusted total compensation including other benefits. As with the numerous examples in other cities, according to Arizona Republic pension spiking in Phoenix has allowed as many as 25 public employee retirees to earn more in their annual pensions than they made in base salary while employed by the city[130].

On December 23, 2014, Pennsylvania Governor Tom Corbett signed into law legislation designed to curb the practice of pension spiking in Pennsylvania that is claimed to save Pennsylvania tax payers $22 million per year over the next fifty years[131]. Despite this lofty proclamation, the new law will only prevent pension spiking for employees hired on and after January 1, 2014. Employees of the state hired prior to this date are not barred from continuing the practice as to their retirement calculations!

Similar legislation was enacted in 2014 in North Carolina. Governor Pat McCrory on signing the new legislation announced *"this law prevents North Carolina state employees from having to subsidize artificially inflated pensions of high earners at the end of their careers"*. For employees hired prior to January 1, 2015, however, these individuals would be eligible to receive the higher pension payments resulted from pension spiking, but the increment would have to be paid by local units of government, not the state retirement system[132]. Of course, this matters little to the North Carolina taxpayer, who is equally responsible for taxes of their local government as they are of the state itself.

The New York Post in an editorial in late 2013 took Andrew Cuomo to task for failing to stop the practice of public employee pension spiking, three years into his term as Governor of the state of New York, after Cuomo reportedly campaigned on stopping the abuse in his 2010 gubernatorial race. The Governor then reportedly claimed that public employee retirement costs had doubled over the prior ten years and were a cause of soaring property taxes in the state[133]. In fact, pension contributions by New York State local governments have risen dramatically from $1.4 billion in 2002 to $12.2 billion by 2012 – an increase of over 650%[134].

The practice of public sector pension spiking was similarly criticized in the State of Minnesota in 2012, but PERA, the Public Employee Retirement Association that manages Minnesota public pensions, claimed at the time that they were at something of a loss to track the practice. They were attempting to combat pension spiking by looking for sudden, large increases in employee salary, but admitted that they don't track overtime, a major source of pension spiking[135]

An audit of the California Public Employees Retirement System covering the period July 2010 to June 2012 conducted by then California State Controller, John Chiang, found that pension spiking, now outlawed in the State, will nonetheless cost state taxpayers an estimated $796 million over the next twenty years. Reacting to the Controller's report, the California Public Employees Retirement System, the agency that manages the investment of public employee pension assets in the state, defended the practice arguing that state law, then in effect, permitted the practice of spiking[136].

When Marty Robinson was elected Chief Executive of Ventura County, California in 2008 supporters cheered her appointment. A councilwoman from the Ventura County city of Oxnard claimed, "That's a glass ceiling broken"[137]. At her retirement ceremony in 2011, her colleagues offered tributes that lasted nearly two hours. The Board of Supervisors renamed a stretch of the County Hall of Administration, "The Marty Robinson Trail". Ms. Robinson's compensation that final year? She was paid a total of $330,000.

Startling as this may be for a public servant, this level of course also forms the basis by which her lifelong pension payments will be calculated. Her highest year compensation of $330,000 entitles Ms. Robinson to lifetime annual retirement benefits of $272,000, an amount it turns out, that is actually *higher* than her base salary for the year of $228,000[138]. By adding unused vacation time, overtime, car allowances and other perks, she was able to significantly raise her final year compensation as the basis for all future pension benefits she will receive in her retirement. While this practice was outlawed by CalPERS in 1999, after numerous reported abuses, counties like Ventura who do not participate in CalPERS, but rather manage their own internal employee retirement systems, are free to allow the practice to continue. In fact, twenty of the state's fifty-eight counties run pension plans that are outside of this CalPERS mandate, following a 1937 law that granted counties a choice between joining the statewide retirement system and creating their own. These twenty counties, known as 37 Act counties, are not required to follow mandates of CalPERS or other statewide directives.

Assuming Ms. Robinson lives to age 85 and the CPI averages three percent over the next twenty years, Ms. Robinson will receive total retirement benefits from Ventura County of *$15,702,608* (or $24,221,167 should she live to age ninety-five). Now here's where it gets interesting. Had she not tried to manipulate the system by spiking her final year income -artificially boosting her salary in the manner described above - her total retirement benefits to age eighty-five would still have totaled *$10,849,000,* placing her in the top 0.01% of retirees. But, apparently, that wasn't enough for this public servant.

Sadly for us, as taxpayers, Ms. Robinson is not alone. Despite a $761 million unfunded pension liability for Ventura County, 84% of its retired county employees earning more than $100,000 per year pre-retirement saw higher income in retirement than they did as employees on the job. The former Ventura County Sheriff is reportedly receiving $272,000 per year in retirement pay (twenty percent higher than his salary) while the former county Undersheriff is receiving $257,997, a full thirty percent above his base due to spiking[139].

Following these and other alarming details of the Ventura County retirement system, a measure was placed on the November 2014 ballot called the Sustainable Retirement System Imitative, designed to stop these and other abuses. Among other reforms, the Sustainable Retirement System Initiative would shift new county employees to a 401(k) style defined contribution retirement plan, thereby relieving county taxpayers of future pension liability for these employees. Proponents argued that the measure could save county taxpayers millions. A group backed by the Ventura county employee unions quickly sued, however, arguing that if such a measure were to be approved, the county would face great difficulty in recruiting new employees (i.e., if their benefits more closely resembled those of private sector employees). Before taxpayers could have a say one way or the other, on August 4, 2014, Ventura County Superior Court Judge Kent Kellegrew ordered the item be removed from the ballot, thus denying taxpayers an opportunity to vote on the proposal[140]. One last thing in case you are wondering. Yes, County judges are covered by the same county pension plan.

* * *

An analysis of state worker salaries in Connecticut in 2012 revealed more than 1,200 employees that earned over $150,000 per year, in a state where the median household income for 2012 was just over $69,000[141]. The Empire Center in New York found a similar story in New York State, where 1,493 state employees, covered by the New York State and Local Retirement Fund earned more in salary than the $179,000 annual pay of Governor Andrew Cuomo[142].

The point here, once again, is not to highlight the excessive salaries of state and local government workers. No doubt, there are some high profile extraordinary cases, like those mentioned above that grab our attention. But the breadth of public employees with compensation greater than $150,000 per year in numerous states, not simply California, New York and Connecticut and that thus serve as the basis for future retirement benefits, is a source of great concern for the future cost of those benefits to local governments and, ultimately, to taxpayers.

In the instance of the Chief of Police of the financially troubled city of Stockton, mentioned above, who upon retiring from the City at the age of 52 began drawing retirement benefits of $204,000 per year, the costs are staggering. Assuming the Chief lives to the ripe old age of 85, and inflation averages 3% per year, his annual retirement benefits due in 2042 will cost the city $541,076. Cumulatively, over his remaining years, total retirement benefits will have cost the City of Stockton and the California Public Employee Retirement System (CalPERS) a total of *$11,776,956.*

CalPERS, to its credit, will invest its assets on deposit to provide for the payment of these future liabilities of the system and will bill the City of Stockton and other California public agencies where the Chief may have worked, for their share of the payments. But any way you slice it, this is a heck of a lot of money. Multiply this future liability by tens and hundreds of thousands of employees, and you begin to get a feel for the enormity of the public employee retirement liability. By the way, in case you're wondering what happens if the Chief lives to 95? Total payments of the retirement system for this one former employee will reach in excess of *$18,000,000.*

At this point you may be wondering how this system could have gone so totally wrong. A reasonable question to ask. To answer it, we must better understand the role of public employee unions and the collective bargaining of public service employment contracts. Collective bargaining is the process by which union leaders, representing member workers, negotiate with employers on the terms of wages, benefits and employment. The practice is far more common in the public sector than the private, with an estimated 35.7% of public sector workers covered by collective bargaining agreements - or roughly five times that of private sector workers[143]. For state and local government workers, the percentage covered by collective bargaining rises to 42%. Perhaps not surprisingly, the median weekly earnings of nonunion workers, according to the US Bureau of Labor Statistics, was only 79% of that of unionized workers.

Oddly, for most state and local governments, the employees on both sides of the negotiating table are often represented by the same unions and covered by the same collective bargaining agreements. Hence, the senior members of staff agreeing or consenting to wage and benefit terms, are often covered by those same benefits. It should also be pointed out that in addition to the benefits afforded by collective bargaining, public sector employees also often enjoy broad civil service protections and the ability to work in a non-competitive industry, where their jobs are not threatened by competitive market forces.

With public employee labor unions emboldened by membership dues and the power over employee wages and benefits, these organizations also play a powerful and often pivotal role in the political campaigns of state and local elected officials. In 2014, the National Education Association alone donated in excess of $22 million to political campaigns. The America Federation of State, County and Municipal Employees contributed an additional $8.8 million. In aggregate, public employee unions donated $50 million to political campaigns and causes in 2014, more than double the level of 2008[144]. Unions have also shown their ability to influence broader issues of public policy, such as the teachers unions' opposition to school choice. This conflict of campaign support and public influence is simply not possible in the world of private sector labor unions.

Be this as it may, our concern here is with the role that collective bargaining has played in successfully negotiating public employee retirement benefits that, in some cases, threaten the economic viability of their employers. A 2002 study showed that since 2002, public sector workers have seen $1.17 in added benefits for each $1 per hour in direct compensation, versus, 58 cents for workers in the private sector. This same study found that today, 86% of state and local government workers have employer-provided health insurance, versus 45% in the private sector[145].

Faced with escalating employee benefits and labor costs and a $3.6 billion budget deficit, Wisconsin Governor Scott Walker challenged the unions in 2011 by promoting Act 10, a bill that would severely limit the ability of labor unions to collectively bargain for (non-safety) public sector employee benefits. Ultimately brought into law by the state legislature, Act 10 limits public labor unions to negotiating base pay only, not pensions, health care sick leave or vacation (oddly enough, Wisconsin was the first state in the country to grant unions the right to collectively negotiate public employee benefits, dating back to 1959). Similar laws to that of Act 10 have been passed in Idaho, Tennessee and Ohio (subsequently repealed) placing limits on public employee collective bargaining.

But now comes the tough question. If all these retirement liabilities have been recognized, how the heck does it all get paid? To be fair, the liability of the retirement system in the instance of the aforementioned pension of the retired Stockton Chief of Police is not $18 million or even $11 million, under current accounting rules and regulations. As CalPERS has certain assets on deposit related to this case, it has the ability to invest those assets to meet the future liability. Not nearly enough assets, in nearly all instances, but under current accounting rules the system can discount the future liability by an assumed rate of investment, and compare this to what assets are now on deposit.

The assets, as mentioned, derive from employer and employee contributions that provide the foundation of support for public employee retirement systems. In some instances, the employee portion of the contribution is actually funded by the city, in some, the employee bears all or a part of the "employee" cost. The annual contributions into the system provide two functions. First, they pay the annual accrued cost of benefits earned by system participants for that year. Typically this is referred to as "normal cost". So "my employees accrued this amount of benefits this year, and I'm depositing this same amount into the retirement fund".

Employer contributions must also amortize any shortfalls in funding status of the plan that arise for any reason including under performance in the investment return on assets, prior years' underfunding, or the consequences of greater benefit concessions. While these accounting requirements constitute sound practices, many municipalities still under-fund in any given year due to budget pressures or in the hopes of "outperforming" financial markets in years to come. However, add up the many years of annual under-funding, mix with sub-optimal investment returns and you come up with a potentially toxic unfunded liability.

Let's take the previously mentioned unfunded liability of the Illinois State Employees' Retirement System of nearly $200 billion. Stop and think about that a bit. With a population in the state of less than 13 million people, that's $15,625 for every man, woman and child in the state, or $62,500 per family of four, just to bring the Illinois employee retirement system back into balance. If you live in the State of Illinois, think about adding this amount to your mortgage or credit card debt. Absent a miracle, you'll end up paying this in increased taxes.

As you might imagine, Illinois while extreme, is not alone in facing this crisis. According to Morningstar, Inc., the investment research firm, twenty-one states have funding ratios (the relationship between investment assets and retirement liabilities) that are below the 70 percent threshold that they consider "fiscally sound". Leading the list of offenders is Illinois at 43.4%, but following close behind are Rhode Island at 49%, Kentucky at 50.5% and Connecticut at 53.4%[146]. Not far behind are Louisiana, Oklahoma, West Virginia, New Hampshire and Alaska, each funded at 60% or below[147].

In addition to these state plans, most states run separate plans for local government employees and public school teachers, each of which face their own levels of funding status. Moreover, while Morningstar attributes a sound level of funding status to 70% and many other governments assess it at 80%, the American Academy of Actuaries in an Issue Brief of 2012, indicates that these levels of funding "solvency" are simply a myth. They argue, public agencies should aim for funding levels of 100%[148].

The problem for these and other state and local governments across the country is not only that pension liabilities have consistently increased over many years, but also that the *rate* of increase has outrun the growth of assets on deposit to address these liabilities. Thus, the unfunded portion of their liabilities has grown and will continue to grow exponentially. According to Moody's, unfunded liabilities of the twenty-five largest public employee retirement systems in the country *quadrupled* between 2004 and 2012. While Moody's attributes part of this growth in unfunded liabilities to lower discounting of future liabilities and lower mortality rates, one startling fact remains. The ratio of active employees who are paying into the system to that of retirees, who are drawing out of the system, continues a rapid decline. This fact is true of public employee pension funds, equally as it is of the federal Social Security system. It is an unavoidable outcome of an increasingly aging society and one of the most troubling factors governing the solvency of public retirement funds.

While public pension liabilities will continue to grow, at some point municipal governments will be forced to "true up" and begin making payments to address these future liabilities. Failure to do so will invariably lead to the prospect of declaring insolvency, or bankruptcy, of the local government. But there is another factor that was clearly at work over the past twenty years in contributing to the growth in public employee retirement liabilities and for that we must look to one of the underpinnings of the 2008 financial crisis.

* * *

NINE

A STICK IN THE SPOKES

Much has been written about the role that debt played in contributing to the financial crisis. From banks to corporate borrowers to consumers, the level of America's indebtedness exploded in the years leading up to the financial crisis. Throughout this period, consumers used debt as a way to leverage their net worth and achieved higher levels of consumption than they could support by wage and salary income alone.

In the period leading up to the financial crisis home equity loans, lines of credit (HELOCs) and cash-out loan refinancing were accessed by consumers in record amounts. At the same time, adjustable rate mortgages, option ARMs and sub-prime loans allowed consumers to leverage home equity for new borrowing in a way previously unknown. According to a 2013 Report of the Federal Reserve Bank of New York, from the first quarter of 1999 through the third quarter of 2008 leading up to the financial crisis, consumer debt rose more than 170%, from $4.6 trillion to $12.7 trillion[149]. Debt secured by real estate, including installment mortgages and HELOCs, accounted for $6.7 trillion of the total $8 trillion boost to consumer debt. While this growth reflected in part a growing population, it also reflected (and helped support) the significant growth in housing prices and home equity. But more troubling, the debt expansion also reflected the lack of real income growth to support consumption along with the preponderance of new financing vehicles that allowed consumers to "bring forward" future consumption.

As credit secured by real estate assets ballooned, so too did the value of the residential housing stock, propelled by the extraordinary availability of credit. While economists have written extensively about the impact of this credit creation on the levels of consumer indebtedness and the prevalence of the securitization market that increasingly held these assets, little has been written about their impact on cities, counties and other municipal governments throughout America.

Supported by the explosion in consumer credit, US housing prices, as measured by the Case-Shiller Index grew by 119% from the period 1999-2007. Moreover, the aggregate market value of US residential housing grew from an estimated $10.9 trillion in 1998 to $28.4 trillion by 2006[150]. At the same time, consumer spending on retail goods and services in the ten year period leading up to the financial crisis, grew at an average annual rate of nearly 3.5%, outstripping the growth of US GDP by more than half of one-percent per annum[151]. By the end of the third quarter of 2007, personal consumption expenditures accounted for 81% of the growth in US GDP.

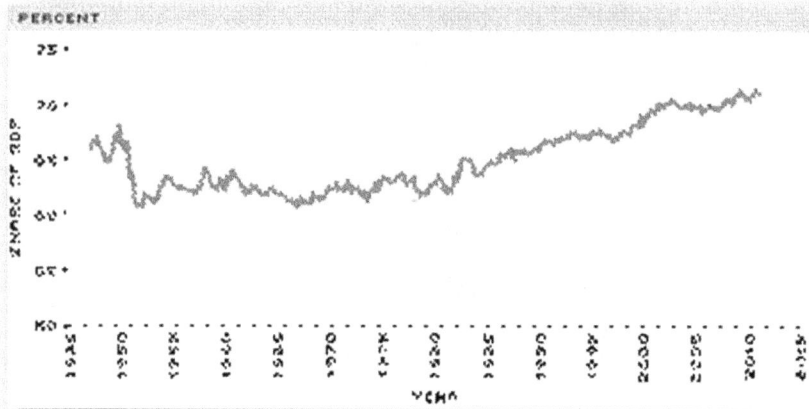

Figure 9.1
Personal Consumption Expenditures (PCE) as Share of Gross Domestic Product (GDP)
SOURCE: Federal Reserve Bank of St. Louis

To understand how this extraordinary growth in real estate values and consumer spending might impact local governments, one must only take a look at how these public agencies fund themselves and provide services to the public. There's no shortage of items that fall under municipal taxes, including business licenses, hotel occupancy, excise taxes on gasoline and alcohol, rental cars and the list goes on. But cities continue to derive the vast majority of their revenue from just two categories: sales and property taxes. While certain cities, like New York, have dedicated income taxes, nationally, they remain the exception. And while the disposition of tax revenue varies among branches of local government and from state to state, the greatest contribution to local government funding comes to cities by way of property and sales tax.

With the explosion of real estate prices and the rapid growth of sales taxes leading up to the financial crisis, local governments unquestionably saw their share of the largess of consumer spending. Total State and local tax revenue in New York State grew from $101 billion in fiscal year 2004 to $134 billion by 2007, an increase of nearly 33% *in just three years*. In Florida, sales tax collections grew by 36% over this same period.

Faced with such rapid growth in revenue over such a compressed period of time and with the prospect of continued similar growth into the future, local governments were under significant pressure to share their new found wealth with municipal employees. In a faculty working paper of the Harvard Kennedy School in 2012, the authors found that from 1998 to 2010, state and local government employee compensation grew by *18.49%*, while private sector employee compensation increased by just *13.36%*[152]. The accelerated growth in public employee compensation over this period further increased the variance between public employee and private sector employee compensation.

Public employee unions were quick to seek increased compensation and benefits for their membership. According to the American Enterprise Institute, benefit increases to New York City pensions in 2000 added $12 billion to the system's costs over the next decade, accounting for 40 percent of the growth in its unfunded liabilities[153].

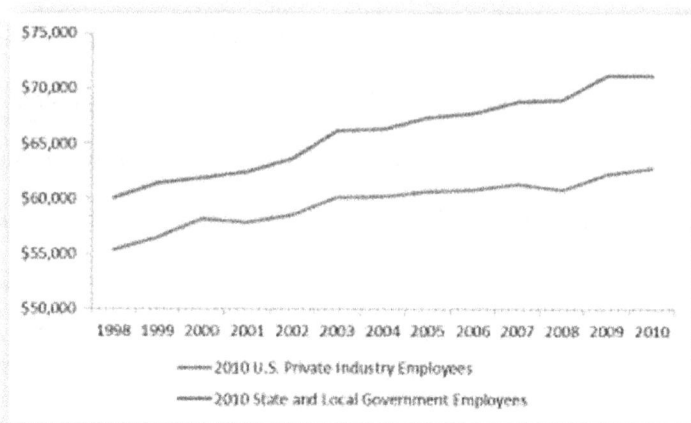

Figure 9.2
Public and Private Sector Average Annual Compensation in 2010 Dollars[154]

In Atlanta, benefit increases passed by the city council in 2001 and 2005 doubled the city's annual required contribution rate from $51 million in 2000 to $119 million by 2010[155]. But Atlanta failed to keep pace with the higher required level of funding. As a consequence, the funding status of Atlanta's police retirement plan fell from 96% funded in 2000 to 64% funded by 2011 (and its firefighters plan from 92% to 61%).

Confronting the challenges of enhanced benefits for City of Atlanta public employees, the city by 2011 was facing a $1.5 billion unfunded liability. With annual pension costs comprising 22% of the city's annual budget, the city proposed and passed a major overhaul of its public employee retirement system. The new initiative would create a "hybrid" plan under which increased employee contributions to the city's defined benefit retirement plan would be combined with a 401(k) defined contribution plan, while increasing the retirement age by two years, to sixty-two. The pension reform would allow the city to tackle its unfunded pension liability while reducing annual contributions to the system by $25 million. When the measure was passed, Atlanta was heralded as the first major city in the US with significant pension reform.

By 2013, however, union workers representing the Atlanta firefighters, police and other city workers challenged the legitimacy of the law, arguing that increased employee contributions toward retirement funding violated the terms of their employment contracts and were, therefore, unconstitutional. In a rare decision to support public employee pension reform, the Fulton County Superior Court in 2014 sided with the City of Atlanta and upheld the constitutionality of its historic pension reform measures. A rare legislative win, indeed.

* * *

I n the years leading up to the financial crisis property values rose appreciably in many communities in the US. The S&P/Case-Shiller House Price Index increased from 86.31 in early 1998 to 189.47 at its peak in the second quarter of 2006. An increase of 119%. While higher home prices were cheered by homeowners (and real estate agents, alike) higher prices also served to boost property tax revenues for many local governments. Total property taxes levied in the State of Florida over the period 2000 through 2007 grew by

103%[156]. Nationally, property tax revenue for local governments topped $107 billion in 2010, from $62 billion in 2000[157].

The widespread availability of home equity loans and subprime borrowings was an effort to leverage this growth in home values by tapping into home equity. Funds accessed by consumers through these borrowings supported greater and greater levels of consumer spending. The enhanced consumer spending greatly contributed to state and local government sales tax collections. All the higher revenue allowed cities to keep pace with growing pension obligations throughout the early portion of the new millennium. But when the housing bubble popped in 2008, property and sales tax revenues soon began a precipitous decline – something that most cities had never experienced before. Suddenly the cities that had agreed to generous employee benefit concessions now found themselves holding the bag and for many, many years to come.

Former City of San Jose Councilman, Pete Constant characterized the situation as follows, *"the city of San Jose over the years has had a situation where, in the good years, as the city was growing and the economy was doing well, you had increasing pay for the employees, and in the years when we weren't doing so well financially, instead of giving pay raises during that time period, they would give increases to benefits." "In a relatively short period of time, our pension benefit was increased from 75% to 80% and then to 85% and then to 90%, in the case of public safety, and that was done all within a decade."*[158]

As with most such benefits increases, the more generous benefits are not merely applied to new employees or even just to the city's existing employees from that date forward. Rather the new, enhanced benefits are typically made *retroactively* for all members of the plan. The resulting impact on the unfunded actuarial accrued liability (UAAL) for the City of San Jose Employee Retirement System is shown below (note – this chart excludes those liabilities of police and fire that are part of a separate retirement system with its own unfunded deficit).

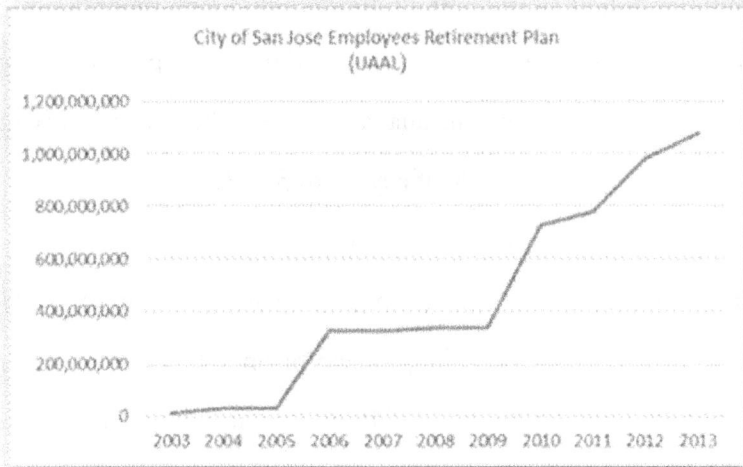

Figure 9.3
Source: California State Controller's Office

Part of the problem may have lied in the spectacular growth in public resources through the pre-crisis boom years. Again, while much has been made of the role that exploding consumer debt had played in leveraging spending and economic growth, little has been noticed of its similar effect upon the finances of state and local government. The problem could equally, however, be a function of the role that local government administrators played in granting further benefits to union leaders through the collective bargaining process; benefits which these administrators, themselves, as state and local government employees often similarly shared.

The City of Rialto, California provided enhanced benefits under its public safety retirement plan as recently as 2008, boosting benefits to 3% of highest year salary at age fifty. The increase in benefits, however, applied not only to prospective employees, but to *all existing safety plan employees*, requiring the city to make "catch-up" payments to avoid having its plan become grossly underfunded. Upon the new formula taking effect, the city's employer contribution rate jumped from 19.3% of payroll to 38.3%[159].

Not only were greater benefits offered to employees, but many local governments failed to keep pace with the actuarial requirements associated with those benefits. Much of the problem of underfunded public pensions in Detroit, Chicago and the State of Illinois became so for just this reason; because elected officials were simply unwilling to make the required annual contributions to keep the systems solvent. In a period of financial stress it was often expedient for these cities to skip or underfund their annual required pension contributions, as did the State of New Jersey in 2014, and for each of the many years preceding. In California, the problem is in part due to underfunding of the annual required contribution, but also due to elected officials giving away enhanced benefits to labor unions who, as a matter of course, contribute actively to political campaigns. Greater than 40% of the contributions made by California cities and counties for police and fire pension benefits in recent years have been the result of benefits enhancements. According to John D. Clark, resources director and treasurer of the City of Garden Grove, California, *"For a medium sized city with 100 sworn police officers and fifty firefighters earning base pay of $80,000 per year, the difference between the old pension formula and the new amounts to $1.8 million a year"*[160].

The results are similar in other major cities, where the rapid turn from system surplus, or overfunding, to system deficit has taken place in a relatively short period of time. In the case of the City of Los Angeles Fire and Police Pension System, the city went from a funding surplus of $345 million to a deficit (UAAL) of nearly $3 billion in a ten year period.

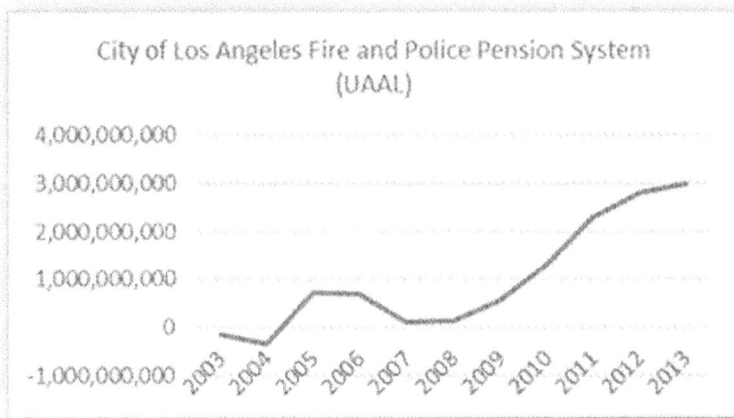

Figure 9.4

Source: California State Controller's Office

The City and County of San Francisco Employees' Retirement System experienced one of the most dramatic turns of fortune in the funding status of its pension plan over the past ten years. From a system surplus of $1.6 billion in 2003, the unfunded deficit of the system had grown to $3.36 billion by 2013, *a loss of just under $5 billion in its funding status in ten years' time.*

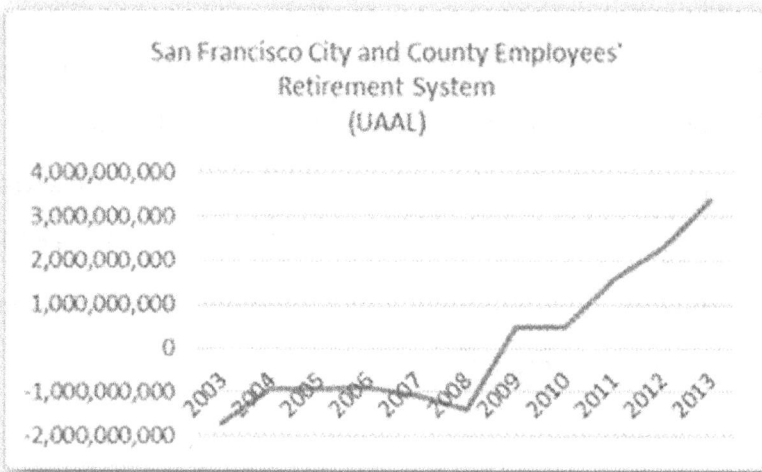

Figure 9.5
Source: California State Controller's Office

* * *

TEN

IT'S NOT ONLY THE ROADS THAT
ARE STARTING TO BUCKLE

In 2014, the State of New Jersey will spend just under $700 million in actual cash contributions to its employee pension fund. The state will spend an additional $2.8 billion to fund retiree health care benefits. The total of these two measures, or roughly $3.5 billion will consume over 10% of the state budgeted expenditures for the year of $33 billion. Despite this significant investment in shoring up the retirement plan of past and current employees, the state will still *underfund* its statutory annual funding obligation by nearly $3 billion.

To fully fund its requirements, just to keep pace with current accrued pension costs – and with no effort to catch up on past underfunding – would require $6.5 billion, or 20% of the state budget[161]. Moreover, by underfunding the state's obligation to the tune of $3 billion, New Jersey has simply deferred this payment, adding to the growing pension gap that must ultimately be resolved by its taxpayers in the future. Citing persistent public employee pension underfunding, the bond rating agencies have downgraded the state's credit rating twice in recent months (following the state's budget decisions) claiming the deferral of pension expense will add as much as $4.2 billion in new liabilities.

A recent report of Alliance Bernstein quantified the annual pension costs, debt service and fixed charges of the City of Chicago at *40%* of its general fund budget[162]. That would mean paying just these items, would require that all the other vital services of the city, including police, fire, sanitation, public works, etc., must all get crammed into an ever shrinking portion of the pie, now just 60% of the total budget.

In its filing to the courts in connection with the bankruptcy of the City of Detroit, Emergency Manager, Kevyn Orr reported that the City of Detroit will spend upwards of 43% of the City's general fund budget in 2013 on just three items: public employee pension costs, post-employment health benefits and debt service. He estimates that in four years, this number will climb to 65% of the general fund, leaving a slim 35% of its total budget to pay for the full range of services that the City provides to residents (as well as for the salaries and health benefits of its current employees)[163]. Of its total debt of $18 billion, roughly half represents pension related obligations.

To understand how this all works, let's introduce the accounting concept of the ARC, or annual retirement contribution. Accounting standards of GASB, the

Governmental Accounting Standards Board, mandate that state and local governments must calculate the annual cost of retiree health and pension expenses that have been earned by employees in that year. The idea is that as benefits vest for employees, annually, the employers – in this case the State of New Jersey – must record the cost of those benefits on its books by funding the ARC.

Despite the GASB accounting requirement, many state and local governmental entities like the State of New Jersey fail to do so, opting instead to make a payment that is far less than the value of benefits that have accrued. There's a variety of reasons for under-funding the ARC, but the most common reason is that there simply aren't enough dollars in the budget to both fully fund the ARC and pay other vital programs and services of the state. So the public agency pays less. In the case of the State of New Jersey in 2014, a total of *$3 billion* less.

Our friends at GASB, however, were wise to the potential for state and local governments to circumvent the accounting requirement. So GASB went on to state that to the extent a public agency under-funds its ARC in any given year, *it must add the difference*, in this instance $3 billion, to its total net pension liability. Now, it's worth pointing out here that for a good number of years no such requirement even existed, allowing states and local governments to easily disguise what their true net pension liabilities were. Local governments would simply fund what was available to them for this purpose in the budget, with virtually no consequence or transparency.

Add it all up, however, year after year of underfunding of the ARC and, in the case of New Jersey, the state now faces a $90 billion shortfall - $37 b in unfunded pension liabilities and $53 b in unfunded health benefits – *or three times the size of the state budget*. And here's the thing, without some economic miracle there is no possible way that the state can "grow" its way out of the problem. Rather, it's the unfunded liability of the retirement system that will continue to grow, as annual pension contributions account for a larger and larger share of the state budget. Eventually, like it or not, tax rates for its residents will increase while services will be cut.

But beginning in fiscal year 2015 the accounting of this liability will change. From this date forward, a taxpayer or creditor will be able to review the financial statements of the state or any other governmental entity and see its net pension liability as plainly as its liabilities for monies borrowed from banks, bondholders or other creditors. Greater accounting transparency will invariably pressure local governments to fund a greater share of their annual costs, or ARC. They will do so, however, from a position of great burden to their budgets.

Following New Jersey's decision in 2014 to (once again) underfund its pension expense in the state budget, Governor Christie defended his veto of the prior budget, claiming the state had no choice (but to underfund the pension expense) if it wanted to avoid raising taxes or undergoing deep cuts to essential services. A flurry of lawsuits quickly followed brought by public employee unions representing teachers, police office, firefighters and other state workers.

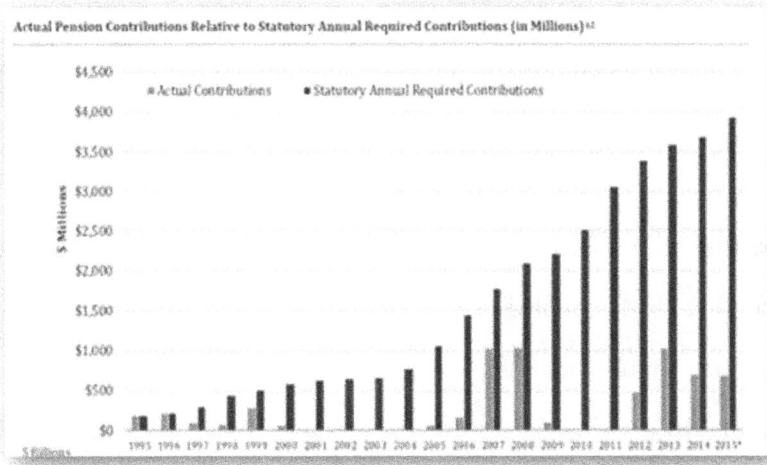

Actual Pension Contributions Relative to Statutory Annual Required Contributions (in Millions)[12]

Figure 10.1

Source: New Jersey Pension and Health Benefit Study Commission

Each challenged the legitimacy of the Governor's actions on the heels of a pension overhaul that the Governor helped design and that required full funding of the plan each year. The courts have recently upheld the claims brought by the labor unions. This is actually quite an important ruling, because it says that not only are pension benefits vested and contractual obligations, but so is the *funding of those payments by the legislature* to the state retirement fund.

But as pension and retiree health care costs rise, as they will, there will be less and less available in the state budget for other services. Pension costs in New Jersey, and most elsewhere in the US, are growing much faster than tax revenue. To put this in perspective, let's take a moment and look at the rate of growth over the past twenty years of the annual required pension contributions in New Jersey. Back in 1996, the state fully funded its ARC. In fact, it was the last year for the state to do so. But the required pension contribution was "only" $200 million. By 2000, the ARC had tripled, yet stood at just $600 million. By this time the state had already deviated from making its required contribution, funding just $100 million of the ARC. From 2000 on, the ARC nearly doubled each five years, to reach its level of $3.5 billion in 2014. The plan now stands at just 44% funded.

As discussed earlier, part of the budget strain that local governments face from pension funding is driven by the assumed rate of investment return on assets held under the plan. Very simply, the higher the earnings assumption going forward, the less the unfunded pension liability appears and, therefore, the less the annual required contribution or ARC that the government must fund to keep current. To understand how this works, think of earnings assumptions as the inverse of discount rates of future payment obligations. If a community is facing $1 billion of future pension payments, the higher the interest rate that is used to discount those payments (or the assumed rate of investment) the less the *present value* of that stream of payments. The lower the present value of a future liability, the lower the *unfunded* portion of that liability, all else being equal.

The inverse of this is also true. If you lower the earnings assumption on invested pension assets (or reduce the discount rate on future payment requirements) you will increase the present value of that liability. In other words, if I owe $1 billion at some date in the future and I invest to meet that liability today at 5%, I will need to invest a great deal more money, than if I assume I can invest the funds at 8%. The unfunded liability can be thought of as the difference between the present value of the assets today and the present value of the future liability.

Put into practice, though, the impact of a lowering of the earnings assumption on municipal budgets can be downright ugly. On October 28, 2014, the board of the Los Angeles City Employees' Retirement System voted to do just this. Under pressure from consultants and advisors, the board voted to lower the future earnings rate assumption on invested pension assets in its public employee retirement system from the current rate of 7.75% to 7.50%. Seems like a small enough change, right? Just one-quarter of one percent. It's hard to imagine that a change of this magnitude would have much impact on the city's budget. But just this small change in interest rate assumption is expected to increase the city's annual budget deficit by *$50 million*. If the rate were reduced to 6% (the rate as argued by its pension consultants as being the more realistic assumption) the impact would *"rip a $566 million hole in the budget"*, according to Miguel Santana, Chief Administrative Officer for the City of Los Angeles[164]. Unfortunately, this same dynamic is being played out each and every day in budget decisions of our nation's communities large and small. It provides a sobering glimpse into just how sensitive municipal budgets are to annual pension costs.

Pension costs also creep into budgets by way of employer contribution rates. As mentioned earlier, local governments must pay into their retirement systems on an annual basis through employer contribution rates, invoiced by the retirement system. While some avoid or defer this obligation, as discussed in the case of the State of New Jersey, any deferrals add to the unfunded position and, over time, begin to snowball. To understand how this works, let's take a look at the two components of employer contribution rates: normal cost and supplemental contributions.

Normal cost pension contributions are generally expressed as a percentage of payroll of the public agency. So if the normal cost contribution rate were 20%, the local government would be required to pay over to its retirement system that year an amount equal to 20% of its total payroll expense for salaried employees. Supplemental payments generally address employer surcharges for unique circumstances like cost of living adjustments, survivor allowances or disabilities.

There are two components to the normal cost. The first part relates to payments necessary to fund the accrued employee pension benefits earned by employees in that year. The second part of the normal cost is a methodology that varies from plan to plan but generally amortizes the unfunded pension liability over some set number of years. The idea is that if a city were to regularly fund its normal cost, over time, the unfunded liability would be paid off over time. So far so good.

But there are many factors that alter this trajectory and cause annual adjustments to the normal cost contribution rate. The first of these factors, as with the calculation of the UAAL, is the investment assumption. If *realized* earnings of the pension system (in this case) are less than forecasted, the unfunded liability will rise. But there are many other factors that also influence this calculation including the actual rate of inflation, mortality rates, additional benefits that may be granted to employees, whether future retirees marry or if payrolls increase at higher rates due to salary increases. Each of these factors will cause retirement system unfunded liabilities to rise, despite what may be steady progress at whittling away at the UAAL through the payment of normal costs. And this also assumes, of course, that normal costs are paid in full each year, a practice as we have shown before that is not always followed.

It is for this reason that contribution rates are calculated by the retirement system each year and billed to local governments. For the State of New Jersey Public Employee Retirement System, contribution rates for local governments have been rising dramatically, from 2% of employee payroll in 2004 to just under 11% by 2012[165]. Contribution rates for various plans –public safety and miscellaneous employees – can vary widely by type and by local government employer. According to a filing by Franklin Funds in the bankruptcy case of the City of Stockton, Franklin argues that contributions rates for the City of Stockton's police and fire system amount to 41% of salaries, an amount that is expected to rise to 57% by 2019[166].

More hikes are on the way. In February of 2014 CalPERS, the largest employee retirement system in America with assets in excess of $277 billion, voted to make changes to its actuarial assumption regarding life expectancies. Increases to male longevity assumptions of two years and to female workers of eighteen months prompted a rate hike of its local government member cities, its third in the past two years. This rate increase, beginning in mid-2016, will cause CalPERS to bill its more than 3,000 public agency members an additional *$1.2 billion per year* through increased contribution rates over the next three years [167]. That amounts to $1.2 billion coming out of California local government budgets, irrespective of the broader issue of addressing any individual local government's funded or unfunded plan status.

The first of its two previous rate hikes, in March 2012, lowered the earnings assumption on CalPERS investments to 7.5%. In the second, CalPERS adjusted rates to allow for faster amortization of unfunded liabilities. The sum of the three rate hikes will raise contribution rates for California local governments by 50% in just three years.

New York State was recently forced to make similar changes to its retirement plans due to a recalculation of life expectancies of retirees. Actuaries for the state plans increased the assumed date of mortality for pensioners by two years, having the effect of increasing the state's annual pension contribution by $355 million. With no room in the budget for the increased pension payment, Governor Cuomo chose to *"borrow"* the payment, essentially deferring its annual obligation, plus interest. Since 2011, these pension borrowings or deferrals have allowed the state to postpone $3.2 billion of required payments to later years. The deferrals, along with investment losses in 2009-2010 have caused the state's annual pension contribution rates to *triple* from 2010 to 2014, while the funded ratio for the state's retirement plan has *fallen* from 105% in 2008 to 87% by 2013[168].

New York City runs its own public employee retirement system, separate from the state. In fact, they run five separate retirement systems for general employees, police, firefights, teachers and non-teaching school personnel. For the Fire Department of New York, pension costs now total $1.1 billion per year, just short of the Department's active duty budget of $1.2 billion[169]. Citywide, New York now spends more than *$8 billion* per year on public employee pension costs. These costs, that now represent 11% of the city budget, amounted to just 2% of the budget in 2000. At the same time that annual budget costs have increased by more than five-fold, the funding level for the city's general worker retirement plan has fallen from 136% in 1999 to just 63% by 2012[170].

* * *

A dding to the woes of local government pension costs are also promised retiree health care benefits. Often referred to as OPEB or "other post-employment benefit" liabilities, many states, cities, counties and local districts are on the hook for health care and other benefits to former employees. These costs come on top of required annual contributions to municipal retirement systems.

While some local governments have granted post-employment health care benefits until age sixty-five when retirees can shift their coverage to Medicare, others districts have offered lifetime medical for the employee and spouse. One of the largest among this latter group is the Los Angeles Unified School District, the second largest school district in the nation with an enrollment of 640,000 students and greater than 37,000 retirees. With $11 billion in future retiree health care costs, the district would have to set aside $868 million in each of the next *thirty years* to fund fully its retiree health care costs (interestingly, this number was quantified as $500 million per year by the California State Legislative Analyst's Office in 2005, with the district then showing a $5 billion unfunded OPEB liability). The district, however, is expected to set aside just $78 million for this purpose in fiscal year 2015 (or less than 10% of the amount required to fully fund its OPEB liabilities)[171].

Statewide in California, the total future OPEB liability, with virtually no offsetting assets to address its payment, has been estimated by former California State Controller (now State Treasurer) John Chiang at $72 billion, as many local governments simply failed to set aside funds to pay for these future benefits[172]. The Employees Retirement System of Texas, in a valuation report prepared by the system's actuaries in 2014, showed a present value of projected OPEB employee benefits of just under $35 billion, an increase of $2.2 billion from just the prior fiscal year. The actuarial value of plans assets available to satisfy this liability, by the way? Zero[173].

Nationally, unfunded OPEB liabilities have been estimated by Standard & Poor's Rating Service to total $530 billion[174]. Rather than pre-funding retiree health care costs throughout the employee's tenure, local governments and school districts often faced with real budget stress - layoffs and cuts to primary services - typically choose to pay the charges annually as they are claimed by retired beneficiaries. Referred to as "PAYGO" systems (or pay-as-you-go) the approach relies upon current revenues to pay the current expense portion of future, long-term liabilities. For the Los Angeles Unified School District, who began offering lifetime post-employment health care benefits in the 1960s, these PAYGO OPEB charges currently amount to $212 million per year.

While CalPERS, the state's public employee pension fund has some $300 billion in assets on deposit to fund future pension liabilities, its retiree health care benefit costs are also largely funded on a pay as you go basis. But with ever-growing retiree populations, longer lifespans and little or no assets set aside, that burden is on a frightening trajectory. As discussed by Kenneth Howse, of the Oxford Institute of Ageing, in a paper of March 2007 *"PAYGO schemes, on this view, are vulnerable to population aging in a way that funded schemes are not. Since the effect of the retirement of the Baby Boom generation will be to increase the ratio of current beneficiaries to current contributors, the schemes are unsustainable in their current configurations"*[175].

From 2001 to 2014, the state's annual public employee retiree health care costs have risen from $458 million, to $1.9 billion[176]. This $1.9 billion annual cost, by the way, does not tackle the broader problem of funding *future* retiree health care liability, but essentially pays the state's portion of annual health care premium for former state workers, currently in retirement. While these payments address promised payments to current retirees, the state's liability for future payments continues to build, growing by $24 billion since 2006 and an additional $7.2 billion in 2014 alone.

OPEB benefits, however, don't typically enjoy the same constitutional protections under state law that have been claimed by public pension systems. In fact, the City of Stockton, in its bankruptcy filing, suspended all post-employment health care benefits for current and former city employees. OPEB benefits were also reduced by the Fresno Unified School District under budget stress several years ago, lowering the district's unfunded retiree heal care obligations from $1.1 billion to $820 billion.

*   *   *

It's not just states and local governments directly that are impaired by these liabilities and that will be increasingly looking for added revenue to address their pension funding shortfalls. In December 2014 the Board of Regents of the University of California voted to increase student tuition at its prestigious UCLA, Berkeley and other state university campuses by a stunning 25% over a five year period. The tuition increases will raise roughly $100 million per year, much of which will be necessary to fund a planned $1 billion addition to the system's employee retirement plan. It is hoped that this contribution, supported by the tuition hike, will stem an estimated $8 billion pension shortfall over a period of twenty years[177]. This story highlights how deep the problem of state and local government pension funding has become and that its reach extends beyond tax increases to homeowners and other taxpayers, but to students and their families attending public supported colleges and universities.

* * *

ELEVEN

401(K)S AND DEFINED CONTRIBUTION
PLANS; THE ULTIMATE HOAX

While the percentage of Americans covered by employer-sponsored pension plans has remained fairly constant over the past 40 years, the mix of those plans has shifted quite dramatically away from *defined benefit* plans, where the employer assumes liability for future benefit payments in favor of *defined contribution* plans, where the employee assumes this liability. Defined contribution plans (401(k)s, 403b and 527 plans) represented only 12% of employer-sponsored retirement plans in 1983. By 2013 that figure had climbed to 71%[178]. They continue to represent the dominant form of American retirement savings in the private sector.

Unlike traditional defined benefit retirement plans, however, where a future monthly pension income is guaranteed by the employer, in a defined contribution plan future payments are entirely uncertain. The level of retirement income is a function of a number of variables including the date of first investment, the amounts invested, the regularity of contributions, and the rate of return on invested funds. In most plans, the individual holder of the account retains election over the investment decisions for the account. Because not all of these variables can be controlled, however, the outcome upon reaching retirement age is highly speculative for even the most diligent and responsible account owner.

In a typical 401(k) plan, the employee elects his or her level of pre-tax payroll deductions or contributions to the plan. Often referred to as "deferrals" these contributions are pre-tax, within certain limits as set forth in regulations of the Internal Revenue Service. Employers may or may not match these contributions, in part or in whole. Even for the richest plans, though, employer matched funds are typically no greater than 6% of salary, while the percentage of companies matching at any level has fallen considerably since the financial crisis of 2008-2009. Employer contributions are also subject in many instances to periods of vesting, with employees forsaking these contributions if they fail to be employed by the company beyond the vesting period. Small and medium size companies, typically offer no matching contribution.

The origin of the 401(k) plan dates back to the Revenue Act of 1978. Signed into law by President Jimmy Carter on November 6, 1978, the Act amended a number of provisions of the Internal Revenue Code including a reduction in marginal tax rates, the widening of certain tax brackets, an increase in the personal exemption and increased capital gains tax exclusions. The Act created Flexible Spending Accounts, allowing citizens to use limited amounts of pre-tax dollars for medical expenses and also, the 401(k) defined contribution savings account.

The Revenue Act of 1978 started out as a modest piece of legislation that followed the broad Employee Retirement Income Security Act of 1974 (or ERISA). ERISA established standards governing corporate pension plans and their administration, as well as a broad set of rules regarding the income tax treatment of transactions undertaken by these plans. The goal of the legislation was to provide US government protection for employees and beneficiaries of company pension plans through mandated financial disclosure of plans, as well as to provide access for regulators to remedies under Federal law. While not requiring companies to establish pension plans, once having done so, ERISA regulates the activities of the plans thereafter.

Historians attribute the broad political support for ERISA to deep public outrage at the time over the treatment of employees during bankruptcy, specifically, the treatment of employee participants in the pension plan of the Studebaker-Packard Corporation following the company's mid-1960s bankruptcy filing. At the time of their bankruptcy, Studebaker was a struggling independent automobile manufacturer located in South Bend, Indiana. The company, along with independents Packard (whom Studebaker merged with in 1954) Nash and Hudson, had all fallen victim to steep price discounting and other competitive pressures brought on by the fierce rivalry of Ford and General Motors.

Studebaker had experienced financial difficulties before, including a trip through bankruptcy in 1933. The company soon reorganized, oddly with the assistance of none other than Lehman Brothers, a company that would meet a similar and spectacular fate some seventy-four years later. In 1959, still struggling to stabilize its finances, Studebaker agreed to a deal with the UAW whereby the company would agree to increase worker benefits, in exchange for the UAW's agreement to allow the company to stretch out the funding of its plan.

But by 1963, Studebaker nonetheless was forced to file for bankruptcy, leaving the funding of its pension plan in shambles. It was the company's filing and, specifically, the actions it would take regarding its defined benefit pension plan that would jeopardize the financial security of thousands of company retirees and outrage the American public. The Studebaker bankruptcy filing and default on its pension obligations prompted a series of investigative and legislative actions, leading to the eventual enactment of ERISA. Despite these legislative efforts, and with no Federal bailout having been offered, the Studebaker bankruptcy would ultimately leave 4,000 of the company's employees with 15% of their plan actuarial benefits while another 2,900 employees would receive no benefits whatsoever[179].

The Revenue Act of 1978, following four years after ERISA, was intended to serve as more of a clean-up bill to the federal tax code, than any attempt to amend or substantially modify US tax policy on retirement. It was designed in large part to limit the use of "cash or deferred arrangement" saving plans (or "CODAs") a tax shelter primarily used by senior executives of large public companies. These plans, dating back to the 1950s enabled executives to squirrel away sizeable earnings on a tax-deferred basis. The plans were generally allowed as long as there was a minimum mix of lower paid to more highly paid employees participating in the program. IRS regulations required that no less than one-half of those electing to participate in the CODA had to come from the lowest two-thirds of employees by compensation. Nonetheless, employers frequently found themselves fighting with the IRS over the plans' tax treatment, as employers strived to stretch the limits of IRS regulatory guidance. The Revenue Act of 1978 was designed to specifically address these attempts to expand the use of CODAs, by formulating a program of broader application.

The 1978 Act went into effect on January 1, 1980 and froze the tax status of CODAs that were in existence prior to 1974, while eliminating the creation of new programs. While achieving this primary purpose, the Act also established a new section of the Internal Revenue Code, section 401(k), under which employee wages, subject to certain limits and conditions, could be deferred to fund a qualifying retirement plan6.

---

6 Similar sections of the Internal Revenue Code were added for public-sector (state and local government and federal) employees (457 plans) as had previously been added for employees of educational and non-profit institutions (403b).

However, in their attempt to restrain the use of the newly created 401(k) by high income senior executives following their recent experience with CODAs, Congress placed limits on the maximum annual salary deferral that could be directed to the new 401(k) plans. By limiting the deferral to some maximum dollar amount or percent of salary, Congress believed that the program would have greater application to the middle class. In addition to the annual ceilings on individual contributions, nondiscrimination requirements were enacted as part of the legislation, to discouraged discrimination of the plan's use in favor of highly paid executives. Companies were required to calculate an Actual Deferral Percentage test (or ADP) each year to provide the IRS with assurance of broad program participation. However, by instituting these limits, particularly the annual contribution limits, Congress unwittingly forced the first of many failures of the 401(k) design: maximum annual contributions, as we will show in Chapter Twelve, would not be sufficient to support the future income requirements of retirees from their accounts.

The 401(k) account is often referred to as an accidental outcome of the Act. The 401(k) as we now know it, was ultimately pioneered by a benefits consultant named Ted Benna, then employed by the Johnson Companies. In developing a benefits program for Johnson, Benna applied to the IRS for certain modifications to the 401(k) account as drafted in the Revenue Act of 1978 that ultimately led to the accounts' widespread adoption by Corporate America. The 401(k) held the principal attraction that rather than wages being taken in cash, income could be deferred by employee election into retirement savings, exempt from federal taxation. The Act further sanctioned the use of salary deductions as a mechanism for plan contributions.

The response was overwhelming. Almost instantly corporations jumped on board, including Hughes Aircraft (1978), Johnson & Johnson (1979) and soon followed by a long list of major companies from 1980-1982, including PepsiCo, Honeywell and JC Penny. These astute employers may have quickly recognized that the potential offloading of a future employee pension liability would not only reduce their companies' annual plan expenses, but would virtually eliminate any negative balance sheet impact of a defined benefit liability into the future. Of course, what burden these companies were able to shed would all too soon become an equal and greater burden upon their employees as these individuals, largely unprepared to do so, would now become fully responsible for investment choices, portfolio performance and ultimately the inherent design flaws of the 401(k) itself.

* * *

C orporations weren't the only ones who perceived the opportunities provided by the Revenue Act. Financial institutions and investment advisors, who aggressively sought to hold these 401(k) and IRA assets, couldn't help but widen their eyes with the prospect of a new and grand source of fee income. Within ten years of the 401(k) going into effect, there were greater than 97,000 company supported defined contribution plans in America, with over nineteen million individual participants[180]. Plan assets had swelled to just under $3 trillion.

Despite the widespread availability of 401(k) plans today, however, roughly 21% of eligible employees *elect not* to participate in their company plans[181]. While this figure has declined from 43% electing not to participate in the early 1980s, it still points to the failing of an elective system of retirement funding. Not only that, but for those who do choose to participate, only 12% do so at the maximum percentage permissible by law. For those earning under $100,000 per year, the percentage that actually fund their 401(k) accounts at the maximum level falls to a mere 6% of plan participants. *For the 94% who fund less than the maximum, their chances of accumulating sufficient assets in their account to support a comparable defined benefit form of retirement fall to nearly zero.*

There are a variety of reasons that can be identified as to why so few individuals participate at the maximum level or at all, including the fact that the struggling economy following the 2008 financial crisis has made savings of any sort difficult for many. The National Bureau of Economic Research (NBER) also points to the losses that many Americans have suffered through passive investment in the stock of their employers, highlighting the ENRON bankruptcy case as a prime example.

The ENRON case poses a thorny problem, even for the governmental guarantee of company pensions that is provided by the PBGC and was mandated under ERISA. While the PBGC can assume the employer liability for employee retirement accounts for those companies entering bankruptcy, it can't guarantee the performance of the investments in those accounts. If for instance, someone were to have fully invested their 401(k) account in ENRON stock and the value of that stock goes to zero, there's little that the PBGC can do under its legislative mandate to make that investor whole. In other words, the PBGC can guarantee pension accounts, but it can't insure against bad investment decisions within those accounts.

And this points to a second critical design flaw of the 401(k). Investment options in many plans are at the discretion of the employee (subject to investment fund alternatives offered) or are otherwise limited to specific alternatives provided by the employer under the terms of the plan. This freedom of choice may sound liberating, but it also enables uninformed and ill-advised investment elections by individuals who really aren't qualified to make such decisions. This is why in so very many cases, like that of ENRON, individuals simply default into purchasing the company stock of their employer. The reasons underlying this flexibility of choice may also stem from the fact that when first introduced, 401(k) plans were thought of as supplements to an employer-sponsored defined benefit plan, rather than as a replacement for such plans. With their basic retirement needs presumed to be met under defined benefit pension plans, employees were thus granted varying degrees of latitude in choosing investment alternatives for 401(k)s.

As a consequence of this free election, though, the NBER has found that employees tend to be "passive decision-makers" choosing the path of least resistance when choosing investment alternatives for 401(k) accounts[182]. The NBER argues that employers have to be especially conscious of how these elections are made, including the default option for investment, and also what options are available to employees upon separation.

For those who do participate in funding 401(k) accounts and invest their balances in stocks, nearly 90% do so through actively managed funds, subject to an average annual fee of 1%[183]. Actively managed funds often under-perform the market indices. For the year ended 2014, and for five and ten-year investment periods ended as of that date, greater than 80% of large-cap mutual fund managers under-performed the S&P 500 benchmark[184]. John Bogle, the legendary founder of Vanguard Funds and a long-time proponent of low fee index funds, warned recently of the dangers in managed fee expenses in reducing retirement plan balances. The US Department of Labor estimated that fees for 401(k) investment management of just one percent per annum over thirty-five years, may reduce 401(k) balances at retirement by as much as 28%[185]. Most people are completely unaware of the impact of fees upon their retirement balances, with fees automatically subtracted from gains before the annual return is calculated.

Another factor contributing to the low funding of 401(k) accounts is the individual's ability to cash out from their plan when changing jobs. An employee leaving a company can roll the balance to another employer sponsored 401(k), transfer the funds to an IRA or take the distribution in cash. The cash out alternative not only raises tax consequences, however, including early withdrawal penalties if prior to age 59 1/2, but it also serves to diminish or eliminate future retirement assets, both by way of the asset itself as well as the compounding of investment returns. Despite the great disadvantage in doing so, one in three 401(k) plan participants chooses this alternative, cashing out an average balance of $14,300 when exiting a job[186].

While average account balances of 401(k)s for those aged 55-64 with defined contribution retirement accounts, as reported by the Federal Reserve, were $111,000 in 2013, balances by income group or quintile, varied quite greatly. Those with incomes over $138,000 per year, reported 401(k) balances of $452,000, while for those with incomes of $39,000 - $60,999, balances were only $53,000. *Moreover, for all income classes, only 52% reported any level of 401(k) account balance*[187].

TWELVE

DID ANYONE BOTHER TO RUN THE NUMBERS?

*"The collective savings gap among working households
age 25-64 ranges from $6.8 to $14 trillion"*

— NATIONAL INSTITUTE ON RETIREMENT SAVINGS JUNE 2013

With all its best intentions of designing a tax-advantaged retirement savings program, Congress failed to engineer around several inherent flaws of the 401(k). Participation by individual election, annual ceilings on amounts that may be deferred, default investment alternatives as well as broad options available for investment selection have all been identified as structural shortcomings of the 401(k). Each of these factors point to the latitude that the program provides employees in their ability to make bad decisions. Bad decisions about when to begin investing, how much to invest and in what type of assets to do so can all contribute to a substantially underfunded retirement account when reaching retirement age. Be this as it may, with only 50% of those eligible for 401(k) retirement plans having actually funded their accounts, the speculation of which factor is to blame is far less important than the outcome.

But, by the mid-1980s experts on retirement planning had already begun to sound the alarm on these and other crucial design flaws of the 401(k). In 1986, in an op-ed piece in the New York Times, Karen Ferguson, Director of the Pension Rights Center expressed her deep concerns with the program. Her principal complaint was that middle class workers, after providing for daily living expenses, would have too little left over in their paychecks to make a meaningful contribution to funding a 401(k) retirement plan. She was largely ignored at the time, amidst an outcry of support for the program by its two main advocates: Corporate America who could now quietly exit the retirement business, and the financial services industry that was licking its lips at the opportunity to invest 401(k) balances. Unfortunately for us all, and especially those middle class employees that Ms. Ferguson described, she was completely correct.

These early criticisms aside, the more compelling and troubling question today is whether under even the best of circumstances, *could* this plan of self-directed defined contribution retirement savings ever have worked? Annual limits to the maximum contribution that could be deferred to a 401(k) account were set early on in the regulations proscribed by the Revenue Act of 1978. Did anyone ever run the numbers to model whether accounts funded at these annual limits, assuming all went perfectly with regard to their diligent funding and investment, could support a reasonable retirement? If so, where's the data? Or was this plan just thrown against the wall by some congressional staffer like cooked spaghetti to see if it sticks? If so, how could Congress be so irresponsible with the retirement future of an entire generation of Americans?

To be fair, it should be pointed out that when the 401(k) was created under the Revenue Act of 1978, Congress may have thought of the program as only a supplement to existing employer-sponsored defined benefit plans. Indeed, in the years immediately following the passage of the Act, many employers did just this. But as discussed in Chapter Six, it didn't take long thereafter for companies to aggressively shed their defined benefit liabilities, either through closing the gates to new employees, terminating future participation by existing employees, or a wholesale transferring of the defined benefit liability to a third party. Perhaps it's only in hindsight that we now see with any clarity that for-profit businesses, burdened by future pension liabilities might seek to exit the pension business given an alternative. Now, it all seems so clear, but perhaps it's not reasonable for us to have expected this level of foresight from our representatives in Washington. But the fact is, as a stand-alone retirement plan, the 401(k) never had a chance.

* * *

There are a limited number of variables that can affect the balance that can be accumulated in a 401(k) or other defined contribution retirement account. As the IRS sets annual limits on the amount that can be deferred pre-tax into a qualifying 401(k) account, the first of these variables, the maximum contribution is fixed by law. The second of these variables is the rate of return which, of course, is neither fixed nor can it be predicted. Fees are also deducted from these returns, thus providing a net (or reduced level of) return to the future retiree. Lastly, we have the element of time, or the number of years in which contributions are to be made, invested and compounded.

Earnings projections must then be measured in relation to yet another set of variables, those that impact the future payments or outflows that are to be made from the account. These variables include the age of retirement, the life expectancy of the individual or both spouses, the rate of draw from the retirement account and the rate of return on the unexpended balance. Lastly, inflation must be considered so as to keep the purchasing power of monies drawn from the account constant in terms of funding future living expenses.

This methodology is not at all unlike that of any other properly managed retirement plan, the defined benefit retirement plans that factored into the bankruptcies of many US industrial corporations over the past twenty years, or the public employee defined benefit plans that today threaten the solvency of many cities and states throughout the country. The goal in any retirement system is to have future plan assets equal or exceed future plan liabilities, or more specifically, to have the income from those assets cover the expected plan outflows. While this is always the objective, as we've seen over and over again for corporations and local governments alike, the people and organizations administering these plans don't always behave as they should. Neither do the people eligible for 401(k) or IRA individual retirement plans. However, 401(k) and IRA plans also suffer from inherent design flaws in a non-actuarially based structure.

Despite all the blame that we heap on prospective retirees for not being frugal enough, or not being disciplined about their savings, *it turns out that an individual would need to begin making contributions into a 401(k) at the earliest possible opportunity, retire at the latest, contribute the maximum amount allowed under IRS regulations, never suffer a period of unemployment, never miss a contribution and make consistently superior choices with regard to the investment of those assets to have any chance whatsoever of accumulating sufficient assets to fund their retirement.* And one more thing, they best not live too long. Here's the math.

First, let's address some recent studies that have attempted to show how 401(k) accounts of greater than $1 million can readily be accumulated over a working career. The most widely reported of these studies was that by Fidelity Investments in January 2014. Fidelity examined 1,000 401(k) accounts in their system, where investors had reportedly accumulated account balances greater than $1 million and earned less than $150,000 in salary. The story was covered by Forbes and CNN, among others. Fidelity pointed to the conventional wisdom of what it takes to build a successful retirement account: start early, save regularly, meet any employer match, invest in equity mutual funds and resist the urge to cash out when changing jobs. All good advice.

Fidelity then gives an example of one of these savers, "Tim", who accomplished each of these saving conventions. He started saving at 25 and retired in 2012 at age 67. He contributed the maximum to his 401(k) account each year, never took a loan and never missed a deposit. Fidelity then references Tim's starting salary at age 25 of $40,000 and his ending salary at age 67 of $73,650[188]. Now, there are a couple of obvious problems with this example. First, if Tim retired in 2012 at age 67 and started working at age 25, then he entered the workforce in 1970. But the Revenue Act of 1978 that created the 401(k) hadn't yet been passed into law. Moreover, the first reported publicly available 401(k) plans offered did not surface before 1980. Let's leave this nuance aside. More to the point, in holding up Tim as an example of how you, too, at home can retire on a $1 million retirement account, let's look at Tim's starting salary. An entry level position today of $40,000 per year, is not considered unusual. But in 1970 when Tim started his career, it was a great deal of money. In fact, $40,000 in 1970 equates to $239,439 in 2012 dollars. So Tim can hardly be considered typical. Let's see if we can get a bit more realistic about analyzing 401(k) accounts.

Take someone turning sixty-five in 2013 who, for purposes of our analysis, we will assume has worked continuously for the past thirty years. That would place the origination of his or her 401(k) at 1984, or about the time that these plans first became widely available through employers. Let's use the maximum annual contribution limit for each year as set forth under existing IRS regulations (for such year) and further assume that this maximum had been contributed to the account in each and every year. Let's also assume that the individual took advantage of "catch up contributions" available to persons over the age of fifty, and began making these additional payments to the account in 2003, at the maximum levels provided.

We'll also assume that the individual employed a recommended 60/40 asset allocation among stocks and bonds, and stuck to it unwaveringly throughout various market conditions (in other words, possessed of a far stronger stomach than most). Further, we'll assume that the individual never withdrew funds from the account or took loans against the balance and earned the rate of return on the S&P 500 (even though index funds that match the returns of the S&P 500 have only existed for a portion of that time - and let's also overlook the fact that only one-third of plans offer self-directed investment). Lastly, we'll assume he or she paid minimal account investment fees (i.e., 1% per annum).

We'll readily recognize this to be the optimal scenario. Our hypothetical pre-retiree would have done everything right from the perspective of today's hindsight: invested every year, invested the maximum amount and made optimal investment choices. Research, of course, would suggest that few if any of us actually behave with such dedication, wisdom and insight, but let's leave that argument for another day. The question then becomes, what could this retiree expect to draw from his or her account for annual living expenses and how long might these funds last?

To answer this question, we would need to develop a model that would project the accumulation of investment balances throughout the working life of the employee and another model to project draw down of those investments in retirement to meet living expenses. Of course we'd need to take into consideration taxes, an assumed rate of investment of unexpended balances and the impact of inflation on actual spending power, or what the withdrawals could buy relative to the dollar's current purchasing power.

First, let's look at the income side of the equation. Favorable stock and bond markets throughout much of the 1980s, 1990s and 2000s have clearly helped our saver accumulate assets. Provided below are investment returns for the S&P 500 and the 10-year US Treasury bond from 1984 through 2013. Note those years where stocks returned 20%, 25%, even 30%. Those returns certainly helped our investor grow his account. Based upon these assumptions and these rates of returns, our dedicated saver would have accumulated a total of $1,003,650.

He would have contributed a total of $335,000 in salary deferrals over thirty years and earned a heck of a lot of interest and capital gains due to favorable markets over most of this period. Bear in mind also, this little nest egg is still pre-tax in the eyes of the IRS, so withdrawals are fully taxable. We should also consider that the S&P 500 went through a period of sixteen years from 1984-1999 with only one year of negative returns and, in that case just -3.10%. That is to say, an investor that had started a 401(k) account in 1999 or 2000 would have experienced an entirely different investment outcome.

Year	S&P 500 (%)	UST 10 Yr (%)	Year	S&P 500 (%)	UST 10 Yr (%)
1984	6.27	11.57	2000	-9.10	6.66
1985	31.73	11.38	2001	-11.89	5.16
1986	18.67	9.19	2002	-22.10	5.04
1987	5.25	7.08	2003	28.68	4.05
1988	16.61	8.67	2004	10.88	4.15
1989	31.69	9.09	2005	4.91	4.22
1990	-3.10	8.21	2006	15.79	4.42
1991	30.47	8.09	2007	5.49	4.76
1992	7.61	7.03	2008	-37.00	3.74
1993	10.08	6.60	2009	26.46	2.52
1994	1.32	5.75	2010	15.06	3.73
1995	37.58	7.78	2011	2.11	3.39
1996	22.96	5.65	2012	16.00	1.97
1997	33.36	6.56	2013	32.39	1.91
1998	28.58	5.54	Average	12.59	5.55
1999	21.04	4.72			

Figure 12.1

S&P 500 and US Treasury 10-Year Rates of Return (1984 – 2013)

All the same, this sounds like an awful lot of money to have accumulated in a retirement account. But let's now take a look at the expenditure side of the equation to see just how long these funds might be expected to last our retiree. To answer this question, we'll need to make a few assumptions about how much he will expend each year for living expenses, and we'll need to adjust this amount for inflation and taxes. We'll also want to make sure to invest the remaining account balance, so that those funds on deposit can continue to grow throughout the retiree's lifetime.

Let's assume that our retiree looks to draw living expenses of $5,500 per month after taxes, above the median income, but nothing too extravagant. But enough to pay monthly household expenses, like rent or a mortgage payment if one is still outstanding, property taxes, insurance, utilities, clothing and food. Maybe there's even enough left over, at least in some parts of the country, to take a few trips to visit the grandkids or head off on a nice cruise.

Let's also assume the current tax rate of 28%, plus average state income taxes of 6%, an inflation rate of 3% and also that unexpended balances are invested at a healthy 5% per annum rate of return. Here's what the retirement account balance will look like over our friend's retirement years.

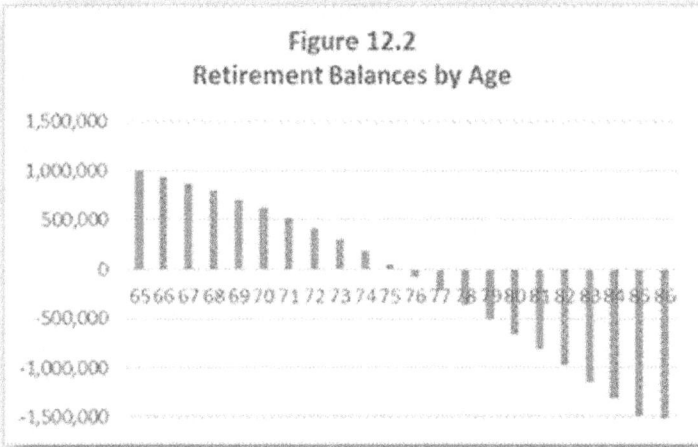

Figure 12.2
Retirement Balances by Age

Our retiree's account will run out of funds in precisely ten years, or by age seventy-five. In fact, he or she would have saved only half as much as would be necessary to fund retirement expenses, assuming our retiree lives to eighty-five or eighty-six. This analysis ignores Social Security benefits, intentionally, which would add roughly $1,500 per month to income (at least until 2033, when the fund is projected to become insolvent).

But maybe we've set up our retiree to live a bit too extravagantly. Let's see what this chart might look like if he cut back a bit, to say US median annual income of $53,000 per year, or $3,037 per month, after taxes. The retiree's thriftier spending would certainly help preserve the balance of the retirement account, with funds now projected to last until age eighty-four. Better, no doubt, but still short of our retiree's current life expectancy.

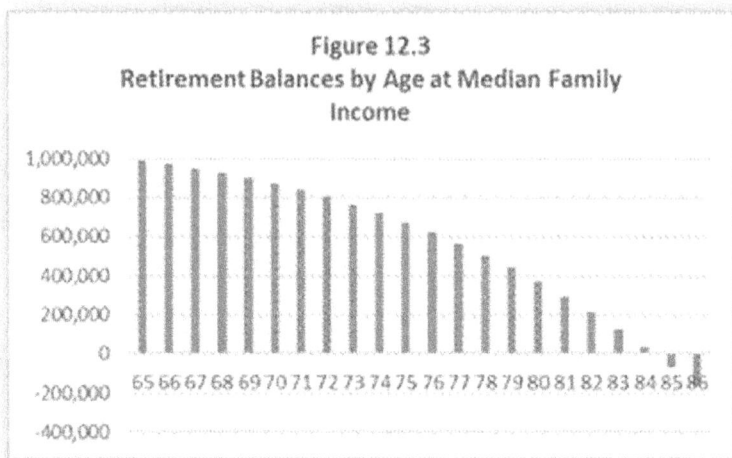

Figure 12.3
Retirement Balances by Age at Median Family Income

It's probably worth taking a moment here and circling back to some of the earliest arguments against 401(k) accounts, including the fact that the middle class worker would not have sufficient funds to make meaningful retirement plan contributions. Our retiree in this hypothetical is assumed to be comfortable living out his or her remaining years on an income of $3,000 per month. Yet, by virtue of the assumptions made to fund his retirement account, our retiree would have had to be employed consistently throughout his working life in a position that paid enough to allow him to fund annual contributions at the maximum level permitted by the IRS. This maximum, including catch up contributions in 2013 was $23,000 per year. So unless our retiree was deferring salary to his 401(k) during his working years at a rate of something like 40%, it's hard to see how his lifestyle in retirement won't take a serious hit.

We must also consider that the historical rates of return on investment referenced above are theoretical, in the sense that our investor would have had to been invested in the pure indices themselves, rather than managed mutual funds. It turns out that the average investor, according to research recently reported by Forbes, earns a far lower rate of return. The average annualized rate of return of individual investors, with assets invested in a blend of stock and bond mutual funds has been just 1.9% over the past thirty years[189]. The factor having the most to do with the actual versus theoretical returns is the buying and selling behavior of investors. People tend to buy stocks and sell stocks at the wrong times. Using a 1.9% earnings rate assumption, however, while still investing the maximum allowable level in each and every year, our investor would only have accumulated $424,696 upon reaching retirement age. An amount that would fund median annual income to only age 72.

What's even more interesting, of course, is that even this account balance is purely hypothetical. We know from data of the Federal Reserve that for pre-retirees, age 55 and over, who had positive IRA/401(k) balances the median value of these accounts was only $111,000[190]. This implies that the average or "median" investors either failed to start funding their accounts at the earliest possible date, didn't max out their annual contributions, missed periods of contribution or failed to achieve the average mutual fund returns of 1.9%. Consider also, this is the median balance for the roughly 50% of pre-retirees eligible for these accounts who have actually *funded* them. This is the reality. But let's return to the theoretical once again to better understand the interplay of each of these factors.

Let's keep in mind, of course, that we are still taking a look at the ideal saver and investor. Someone who has saved in each and every year at the maximum levels permitted by IRS regulations and invested optimally, with no withdrawals. Now let's see what happens in retirement if this perfect investor is a bit less fortunate with the returns on his account after entering retirement. He starts with the same balance accumulated over thirty years in his 401(k) and withdraws funds conservatively in retirement at the median income level of sustenance. But now let's assume rather than a five percent annual return in retirement, our retiree, perhaps a bit more cautiously only sees a return of two percent per annum. That mere reduction in investment rate of earnings from five to two percent will shorten the period of the individual's retirement funding by five years, to age 79, or just fourteen years after entering retirement.

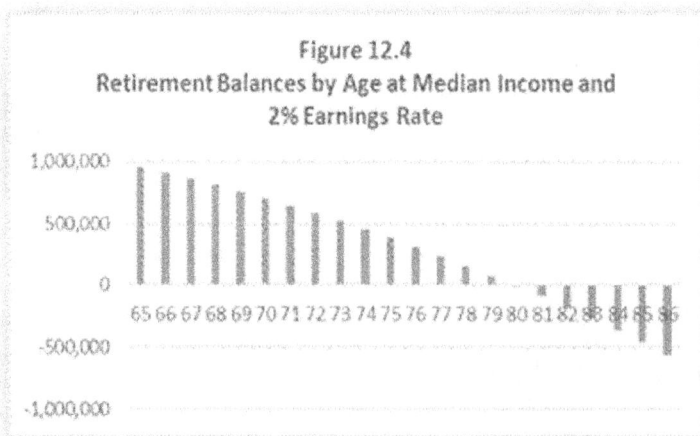

Figure 12.4
Retirement Balances by Age at Median Income and
2% Earnings Rate

Inflation would also be highly detrimental to our retiree. Even on median income and enjoying five percent per annum investment returns, an inflation rate of five percent per annum would leave our retiree broke by age eighty-one.

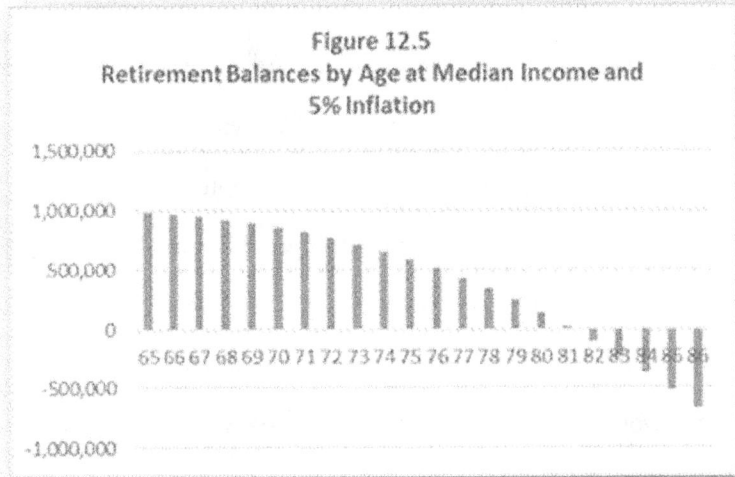

Figure 12.5
Retirement Balances by Age at Median Income and 5% Inflation

This may have the reader feeling somewhat unsettled about their own levels of contributions assuming like most everyone, they haven't always done everything exactly right. Perhaps they waited a few years before beginning a 401(k) plan, or didn't invest each year, or deferred less than the annual maximum. Or perhaps due to unemployment or hardship, they skipped a number of years in funding their accounts. Maybe they weren't as expert as they would have liked in executing their investment strategy or invested too heavily in bonds. So let's take a look at the less than optimal investor, someone more like us.

Investment selection, it turns out, is critical. An investor under precisely the same set of assumptions who was invested entirely in bonds, would not have fared quite so well. For this retiree, living on median US family income, in a low inflation environment, with a retirement portfolio earning 5% per annum, the future would not look nearly as bright. He would have still done quite nearly everything correctly in his years prior to and in retirement. He would have started his 401(k) contributions early, never missed an annual contribution in thirty years, and made the maximum contribution in each and every year. His more conservative investment philosophy, however, would mean that the value of his retirement account at age sixty-five would now be worth only $601,706. Still a reasonably large number, but the funds would only last him for the first ten years of his retirement.

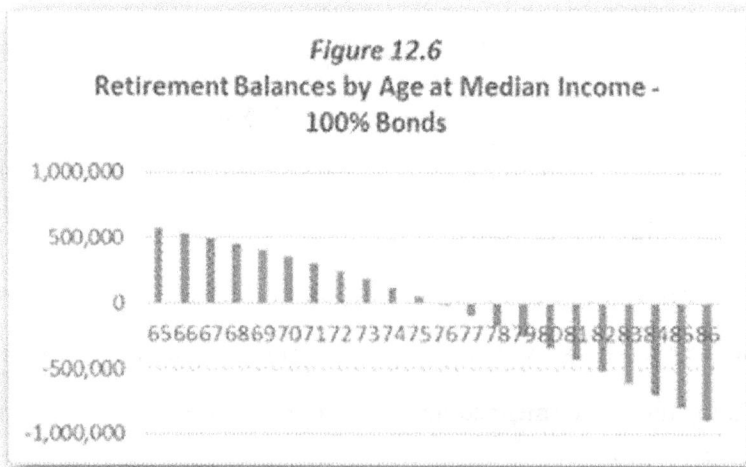

Figure 12.6
Retirement Balances by Age at Median Income -
100% Bonds

Lower investment returns in his retirement years, or higher inflation would, of course, eat away at these savings and bring the date of depletion much closer. This more conservative investment approach would have turned out to be a complete disaster for the retiree that was hoping to live on a slightly higher budget of $5,500 per month, after taxes. For this retiree, his fully funded retirement account would barely last him to age seventy.

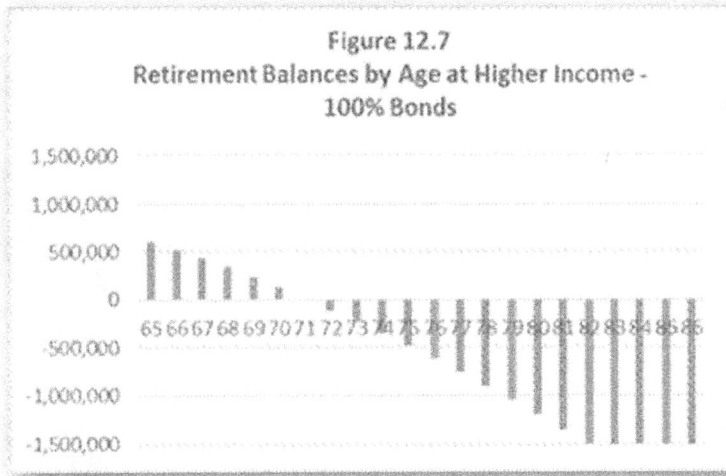

Figure 12.7
Retirement Balances by Age at Higher Income -
100% Bonds

While a less than optimal investment choice is clearly detrimental to 401(k) retirement funding, so is the decision as to what level of annual salary to be deferred to fund the account and when to begin. Electing to defer salary into a 401(k) account at less than the maximum permitted by IRS regulations has a devastating impact on the future retiree's ability to fund his retirement.

Reducing contributions by one-half of the IRS maximum, while beginning contributions at the earliest possible date, continuing to make those contributions in each and every year for thirty years, providing the optimal investment of the account and taking no withdrawals or loans, cut the length of time our retiree could fund living expenses considerably. Even attempting to live within a monthly budget of roughly $3,000 per month, our retiree's account will be exhausted before he turns seventy-five.

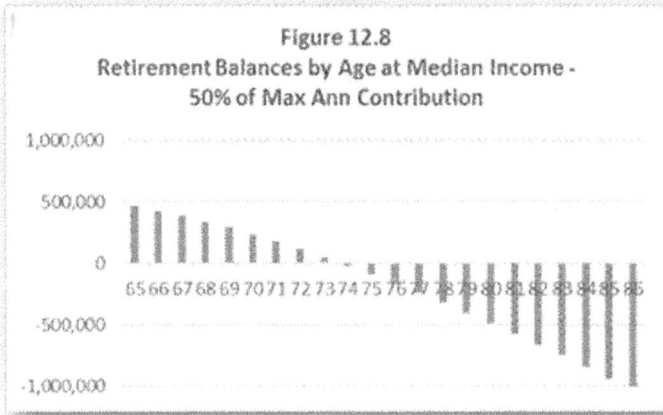

Figure 12.8
Retirement Balances by Age at Median Income - 50% of Max Ann Contribution

The only factor seeming to have little real impact on the longevity of the funding provided by the retirement account turns out to be the funding of "catch up" payments for individuals fifty and over.

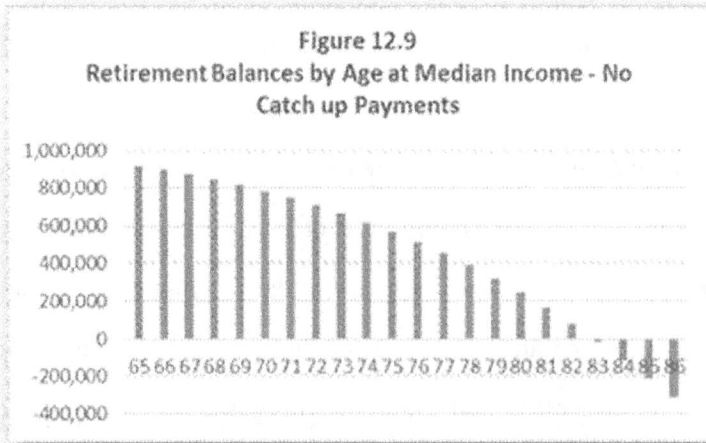

Figure 12.9
Retirement Balances by Age at Median Income - No Catch up Payments

It appears that the limited additional salary deferral for the catch up contribution (currently $5,000 per year) plus the fact that the catch up payments come so close to the date of retirement and therefore, benefit the least by the compounding of investment returns, implies they are of relatively limited value in extending the funding of the retirement account. Our retiree drawing median income could fund his living expenses until age eighty-two, without having made catch up payments during his working years, or just two-years earlier than if he had.

Delaying the start date of participating in a 401(k) is perhaps the most significant reason why actual 401(k) balances and those theoretical accounts discussed above, ultimately diverge. Delaying funding, it turns out, has the greatest impact of all the variables considered, on the total account accumulation or the value of the account in providing for retirement expenses. This factor highlights the third of the great flaws of the 401(k) design: *the fact that contributions are voluntary.*

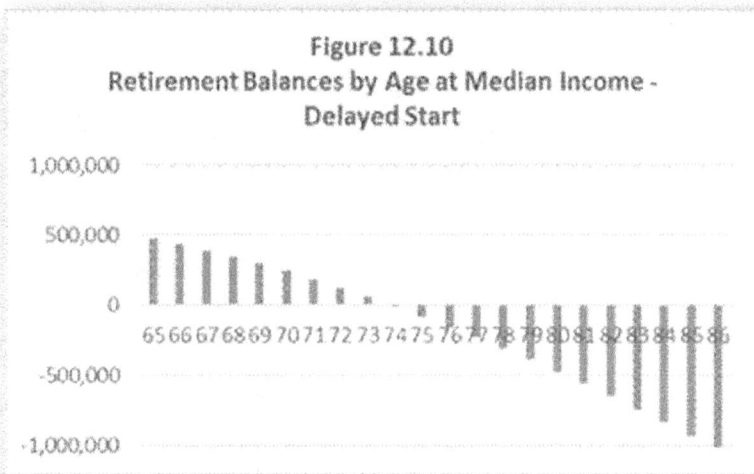

Figure 12.10
Retirement Balances by Age at Median Income - Delayed Start

Delaying participation in a 401(k) is one of the most likely reasons why the median balance of those approaching retirement age with 401(k) accounts is only $111,000[191], rather than the hypothetical optimal balance of one million dollars discussed above. In our modelling, the employee who delayed funding his or her 401(k) account for ten years, even if funding thereafter was at the maximum allowed by law, was consistent throughout the remaining term, with optimal investment of the balances, would still see the balance of this retirement account fall by half and provide funding at the median income level to only age seventy-four. *Missing the first ten years of investment has about the same impact on retirement funding as having contributed just one-half of the IRS maximum over the entire 30-year period.*

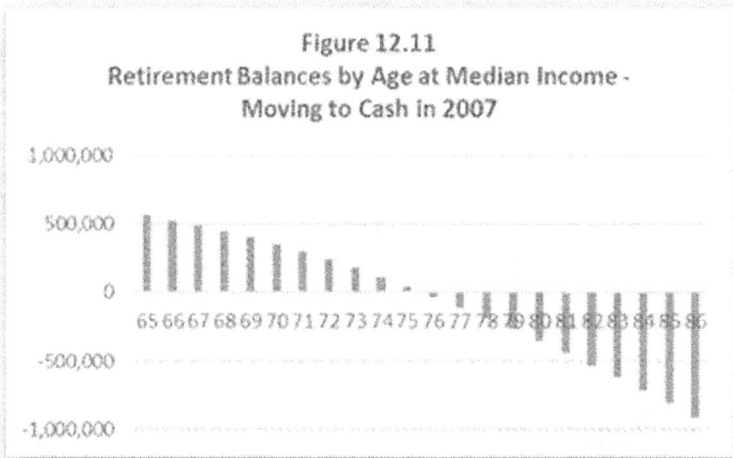

Figure 12.11
Retirement Balances by Age at Median Income -
Moving to Cash in 2007

All too similar is the effect of having changed investment elections following the devastating losses following the 2007-2008 financial crisis. Investors who moved their investments to cash or money market funds in early 2008, will have seen the accumulations of their accounts suffer greatly, compared to our base case. In this instance our retiree, drawing median income would see his retirement account last until age seventy-five, nearly ten years earlier than if he had remained fully invested.

These results exclude any amounts funded under 401(k) plans by way of employer match, as well as those few extraordinary investors who may have "beaten the market" by individual stock selection, by timing the market or by investing in company stock of those select companies that were takeover candidates or otherwise outperformed the market. Leaving these outliers aside, however, the modelling of the hypothetical 401(k) accounts above tells us much about why actual investor balances in 401(k), 403(b), 457 and IRA accounts differ so dramatically from the theoretical possibilities of these accounts. It also helps us address the troubling question of why only half of people to whom a 401(k) is available have opted to fund it. And why for those who have funded 401(k) accounts, the median balance is only $59,000.

But it also helps answer the question of whether the 401(k) account, as designed under the Revenue Act of 1978 *could ever have worked*, given its seemingly obvious design flaws of voluntary participation, employee self-directed investment and the lack of a prudent employer default option. But more importantly, did it require nothing less than optimal performance under all variables and conditions that could influence its results? Dual-income households will certainly improve on the results over households with one working member and one retirement account, but is it really reasonable to design a retirement system that *requires* a dual-income household to produce adequate retirement savings? This is especially of concern, given that the percentage of American households reporting as dual-income, despite gains over the past thirty years, make up only about one-third of total households[192].

Here's what we do know. First, failing to participate in the funding of a 401(k) from the earliest possible age is devastating in its impact on the ultimate funding of the account, as is failing to fund the account in each and every year or at the maximum level. Second, 401(k) retirement funding is highly subject to investment selection, something that by its very nature cannot be known with forethought. Third, during retirement, inflation and the return on unexpended balances, two other uncertainties, can have a dramatic impact on the account's ability to fund retirement expenses.

We have also learned, though, that even under the best of all possible circumstances with optimal foresight and dedication, the 401(k) by itself can only sustain an income of moderate means, roughly $3,000 per month, and then, to a point of only twenty years into a typical retirement. That would argue that the 401(k), by all measures, is a dismal failure as a retirement plan of broad application for Americans.

*   *   *

THIRTEEN

LET'S NOT LEAVE THIS TO PRAYER

I t's become fashionable these days when referring to Social Security to claim that the program was "never meant to be the sole source of income in retirement", but rather was created as a supplement to other retirement savings. Say something enough times and it finds a way of becoming fact. A 2014 handbook on "Understanding the Benefits" of Social Security produced by the Social Security Administration is quick to point out this "role" of Social Security benefits serving as a supplement to other retirement income. This insight is also shared in the findings of Senator Harkin's Senate Committee on Health, Education, Labor and Pensions, as a premise in putting forward the Committee's proposed USA Retirement Accounts[193].

It's hard to say where or how this concept originated or who first uttered these words. Perhaps this is the normal process by which history is reinterpreted to fit modern facts and circumstances. Or perhaps this characterization of Social Security's intent is simply a crude dodge of our elected officials, unwilling to bear any responsibility for the system's shortcomings. Either way, the statement is entirely untrue.

Social Security found its origins in America as a safety net for veterans, first those veterans of the Civil War, at least those of the Union Army. This retirement safety net was broadened in 1890 to include all veterans aged sixty-five and older and, then broadened again in providing care for the disabled and, more generally, for the elderly for whom poverty had become so widespread during the Great Depression. By the time the Social Security Act was signed into law by President Roosevelt, it included not only the Social Security system as we now know it today, but also old-age assistance or public relief (under Title 1 of the Act) unemployment insurance, aid to dependent children and aid to states to support medical insurance for the elderly[194].

In Roosevelt's speech to Congress in 1934 in delivering the Act, he makes the point of the social security system serving as a safety net for the elderly and unemployed eminently clear,

"We can never insure one hundred percent of the population against one hundred percent of the hazards and vicissitudes of life, but we have tried to frame a law which will give some measure of protection to the average citizen and to his family against the loss of a job and against poverty-ridden old age."

Nowhere in his speech or in other communications of the President or the Committee on Economic Security (CES) charged with drafting the Social Security Act is there any mention of this concept of a Social Security program offered to all, as a supplement to other retirement income. Moreover, implicit in this modern day view of Social Security's intent is the premise that Social Security benefits are entitlements, not unlike dividends for those who have "invested" in the Social Security system. Yet despite the divergence from historical record, this simple common notion remains: if you pay into Social Security through FICA payroll deductions throughout your working career, upon turning sixty-five you are *entitled* to draw benefits from the system proportional to your contributions.

An extreme example of this widespread belief can be found in the US Supreme Court Case of Flemming vs. Nestor (1960). Mr. Nestor, a private individual, sued the Secretary of Health, Education and Welfare for unpaid retirement benefits. Nestor, you see, had been deported for having been a member of the Communist Party and following the subsequent denial of his Social Security benefits, sued for restitution. Interestingly, Mr. Nestor took this action despite a 1954 law specifically requiring the Social Security Administration to deny benefits to anyone having been so deported. His appeal centered on the argument that Social Security benefits were a contract, which Congress by way of the 1954 law could not break. The court, however, found that Nestor's denial of benefits was upheld, despite him having paid into the Social Security system via payroll deductions for a period of nineteen years. In what is considered a landmark ruling, the court ruled that Social Security benefits were in fact not contractual and, therefore, not an *entitlement* available to all who had so contributed to the system.

The Social Security Administration characterized the findings of the court by writing,

> *"There has been a temptation throughout the program's history for some people to suppose that their FICA payroll taxes entitle them to a benefit in a legal, contractual sense. That is to say, if a person makes FICA contributions over a number of years, Congress cannot, according to this reasoning, change the rules in such a way that deprives a contributor of a promised future benefit. Under this reasoning, benefits under Social Security could probably only be increased, never decreased, if the Act could be amended at all. Congress clearly had no such limitation in mind when crafting the law. Section 1104 of the 1935 Act, entitled "RESERVATION OF POWER," specifically said: "The right to alter, amend, or repeal any provision of this Act is hereby reserved to the Congress." Even so, some have thought that this reservation was in some way unconstitutional. This is the issue finally settled by Flemming v. Nestor."*

Despite a Supreme Court ruling to the contrary, this widely-held but mistaken view of the original intent of the Social Security Act continues to pose one of the most fundamental problems we now face in addressing America's retirement crisis: the belief that Social Security benefits are an entitlement that one *earns* throughout their working career.

But let's pause here and travel back once again to the creation of the Social Security system under the Roosevelt administration. The CES in designing the Act in 1934 envisioned a system where the government would function as a plan administrator, with workers contributing to a self-supporting system. There was dissent in this view, however, as seems to have always existed in Washington even within administrations, with some members of the CES supporting the use of general tax revenues to help fund the program. President Roosevelt, for his part, was committed to the idea of Social Security being modeled on the European concept of "social insurance" whereby a program, supported by employers and employees with *"no money out of the Treasury"*, could ultimately lessen the government's role in providing general relief and old age assistance. Unfortunately this "crossover" point or full hand-off from government support to the private sector (per the actuarial tables of the CES that followed) was not projected to actually take place until 1980, or some forty-five years after the adoption of the Act.

In the words of President Roosevelt to Congress in 1934 when promoting the Act, his words spoke only of a safety net for the elderly. In the President's remarks he said,

"Security was attained in the earlier days through the interdependence of members of families upon each other and of the families within a small

community upon each other. The complexities of great communities and of organized industry make less real these simple means of security. Therefore, we are compelled to employ the active interest of the Nation as a whole through government in order to encourage a greater security for each individual who composes it . . . This seeking for a greater measure of welfare and happiness does not indicate a change in values. It is rather a return to values lost in the course of our economic development and expansion."

We now know, of course, that Roosevelt's intent of self-funded social insurance, as to the future of the current Social Security program will no longer be possible, at least not without either substantial increases in the payroll tax rate, greatly reduced benefits, or both. But more importantly, this widely-held premise of an exclusively self-supporting social security system will turn out to be the second of our greatest challenges in finding a solution to the modern retirement crisis.

It's also worth pointing out that the retirement crisis is not at all unique to America. According to the Organization for Economic Development and Cooperation ("OECD") overall pension costs now account for 17% of total public spending in OECD countries, with the *"pension landscape changing at an astounding pace over the past several years"*. Some countries, such as Italy, now spend as much as 30% of all public spending on pension contributions[195]. The distribution of that spending, however, varies considerably with many OECD countries funding a high percentage of these costs at the federal, or sovereign level. For the US, pension costs are spread throughout the entire economy including local government, the corporate sector and private individuals. The federal government's role, however, has largely been limited to Social Security, a system that continues its attempt to operate as a self-funded enterprise through dedicated payroll taxes.

It's also time we stop simply blaming the retirement crisis upon those approaching retirement for having saved too little. Let's resist the temptation to castigate Baby Boomers approaching retirement for being profligate in their spending throughout their working lives, and failing to properly prepare for retirement. *Bear in mind, this is the first generation in modern times who bore the primary risk and responsibility for retirement savings directly.*

Further, for quite some time, governmental programs and economic incentives have not been aligned to promote the income gains necessary for the average American to actively save. Median family income in the US has actually *declined* each year since the 2007 financial crisis[196]. Median income now stands $5,000 or eight percent below its level of 2007. In fact, as shown by the chart below of US Census data, median family income, when adjusted for inflation, is back to where it was in 1989.

In an effort to make ends meet, an estimated one-third of those between the ages of 18-30 have returned home to live with their parents to lessen the financial burden of living on their own. Hardly an environment to promote retirement savings.

With incomes stagnant and college tuition growing at nearly twice the rate of inflation, it has been difficult, if not impossible, for many families to contribute to retirement savings plans. Moreover, not only have we failed as a society to sufficiently promote a rising standard of living among the middle class that would facilitate a higher rate of savings, but Congress in 1978, wittingly or otherwise, felt it appropriate to transfer the burden of future retirement savings from employers to employees through the creation of IRAs and the 401(k).

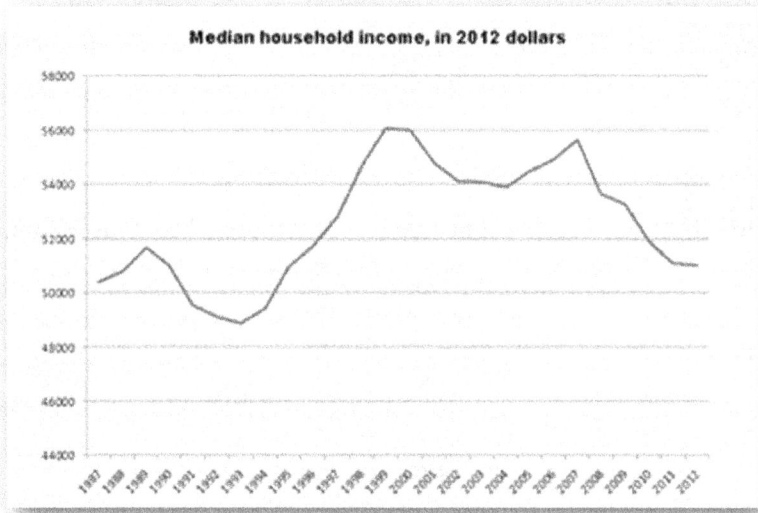

Figure 13.1
U.S. Census, 2014

Former President Bill Clinton reported at the recent Clinton Global Initiative that there are three reasons why median income hasn't increased. The first, according to Clinton is that weak labor markets and a failure to raise the minimum wage have forsaken income gains. The second, is our limited ability to create more profitable positions. Lastly, the sluggish economic environment of the past several years has failed to promote the demand for labor and growth. To this last point, and with great insight, Clinton points to the increasing use of corporate cash flow to fund management pay packages, stock buybacks and increased dividends rather than capital investment that would lead to further employment and consumption.

Each of these points is true. But there are other factors as well at work in the economy that have derailed wage gains for the average American. The exporting of jobs to less expensive foreign labor markets has clearly played a role in devaluing the contributions of American workers. At first limited to unskilled labor, assembly work and the like, increasingly even highly skilled positions are finding their way to foreign shores. The Wall Street Journal reported that as of 2011, US multinational corporations employed 21 million people at home and slightly greater than 10 million abroad. In the early 2000s, these companies downsized their employment in the US by 2.9 million workers while increasing their hiring abroad by 2.4 million[197]. The companies exporting these jobs were in many cases high flying tech firms like Oracle, Cisco and Microsoft. Cisco added 21,000 employees abroad in the five years leading up to 2011, while adding just 10,000 in the US. By the end of 2010, 63% of Oracle's employees were located overseas.

The stubbornly high rate of unemployment and the underemployment of Americans has also exerted downward pressure on wages. An excess supply of labor creates intense competition for each and every position that becomes available. With the power shifting so strongly to employers, job seekers have little negotiating power over salaries. Workers have had to accept part-time jobs, typically for low wages, just to stay employed. In so doing, they have been removed from the ranks of the unemployed for purposes of measuring the U-3 unemployment rate, despite the fact that they would prefer full-time employment at greater wages.

A report prepared by Global Insight for the US Conference of Mayors found that jobs that had been created over the past five years, on average, paid *23% less than those lost during the 2008-2009 recession.* Total wages lost in the move to lower paying jobs were estimated at $93 billion. The same phenomena was observed in the recovery from the 2000-2001 recession, where the annual wage of jobs created in the period following the recession averaged $5,000 or 12% less than those lost *in the same sectors* in the 2000-2001 recession.

In the 2008-2009 recession, where 8.7 million jobs were lost, the annual wage of jobs lost was $61,637. In the recovery that followed, the average wage of new jobs created averaged $47,171, or $14,500 less than similar jobs held prior to the recession[198]. While the greatest number of jobs were lost in the manufacturing and construction sectors, the highest number of new jobs created were in the relatively low paying industries of food and beverage, health care and social assistance. These workers, though employed, are taking fewer vacations, eating out at restaurants less often and spending less on clothes, health care and other essentials.

Others in the workforce have been *forced* into early retirement. While many young people might claim they never plan to retire, the data shows that things don't always work out according to plan. Older workers, many of whom might have anticipated working until their late sixties or to seventy are often forced to leave the labor market, in some cases in their mid-fifties due to layoffs, injury or disability. In 2009, the year following the financial crisis, applications to the Social Security Administration for retirement benefits increased by 22% over the prior year, surpassing by wide margin the 15% increase the SSA had projected, based upon their demographic models. The variance was attributed to the poor labor market[199].

While the number of workers who predict they will retire past sixty-five has been growing over the past twenty years, the median age at which workers *actually* retire has held fairly constant at sixty-two. Only 9% of workers now say they plan to retire before sixty, *while 37% actually do*[200].

Faced with a labor market of stagnant wages, a corporate culture that is sending jobs overseas, reluctant underemployment, the replacement of higher paying industry jobs with lower and the forced early retirement for many, it's hard to so cavalierly fault these individuals for failing to max out their 401(k) contributions throughout their working careers.

The increasing role of automation and robotics in manufacturing has also served to limit wage gains, as have increasing regulatory burdens on employers. Perhaps most importantly, though, is the role of the Federal Reserve Bank, post-crisis, in unwittingly shifting the balance of income in the economy from labor to capital. A 2012 report of the Federal Reserve Bank of Cleveland found that labor's share of total income had fallen from 64% of total income in 1999 to just 58% by 2012. A substantial portion of this decline happened in the years following the financial crisis. Not surprisingly over the ensuing years, with median income stagnant and stock wealth growing, the wealth gap between rich and poor has risen steadily since the financial crisis of 2007.

A report of the Pew Research Center in late 2014 found that the wealth gap between middle and upper income families in America had reached an all-time high, with the median wealth of upper income families now at 6.6 times the median of middle income families. This disparity was far wider when comparing upper income to lower income families, with upper income median wealth at 70 times that of lower income families. This data represents the widest gap in the thirty years the Federal Reserve Bank has been compiling this data[201].

While the Fed has tried to assist the economic recovery through ultra-low interest rates and its program of quantitative easing, economists are now questioning what impact these polices have actually had on economic growth and wage gains. The Fed's ultra-low interest rate policies have been predicated upon the belief that by lowering the cost of capital in the economy, private businesses and consumers alike would benefit from lower borrowing costs. Lower borrowing costs, the theory goes, would spur the use of debt fueling the growth of investment and consumption, thereby boosting GDP. But it hasn't quite worked out that way. Not even close.

A 2012 report of the Federal Reserve Bank of St. Louis pointed to fore-casted weak consumer spending in the years ahead[202], while an article in the Wall Street Journal that same year claimed that capital investment of US companies had fallen off a cliff. Half of the country's largest public companies had announced plans to shrink capital spending on buildings, equipment and even software. According to The Wall Street Journal, they took this action in response to uncertain demand for goods and services in the economy, opting to flow excess cash into dividends and stock buybacks[203].

Compounding the inefficiencies of capital allocation brought on by the policies of the Fed, Congress also passed the Dodd-Frank Act in July of 2010, largely in reaction to the bankruptcy of Lehman Brothers, the demise of Merrill Lynch and Bear Stearns, and the perceived role these and other money center banks played in contributing to the 2008 financial crisis. Now in varying stages of implementation, we are just beginning to learn of the impact of Dodd-Frank upon the banking sector. Designed to help create a level playing field in banking and the broader allocation of credit resources across the economy, we are now finding that Dodd-Frank is having precisely the opposite effect on the banking sector and the economy.

While intended to bolster the community banking sector that has traditionally led in providing small business, agricultural and energy loans, the
number of community banks has fallen to 6% of the "C&I" loan market or
loans to commercial and industrial companies since 2010, down from 12% in
2006, prior to the adoption of Dodd-Frank[204]. Community banks' share of
these C&I loans has fallen greatly, while those of the larger banks have risen
significantly over the same period. This pattern follows the swift decline of
community banks following the Riegle-Neal Interstate Banking and Branching
Efficiency Act of 1994, a bill that authorized and encouraged interstate banking mergers.

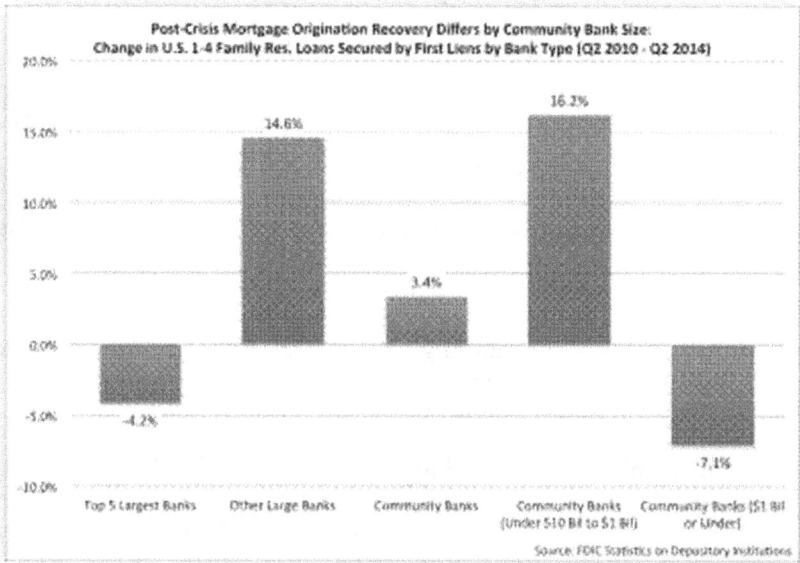

Figure 13.2
Source: Harvard Kennedy School 2015

Overall, community banks' share of total banking assets has fallen from 40% in 1994 to 20% today. Despite the role Dodd-Frank has played in increasing regulatory burdens of the sector and in diminishing these banks' role in C&I lending, community banks still provide greater than 50% of small business loans and 77% of all agricultural loans in the US. Their intimate knowledge of local markets for agricultural products and residential real estate also result in significantly lower default rates for the loans these banks originate, relative to the larger banks.

Despite these benefits to the economy, their role in lending to consumers and small businesses continues to diminish. According to a recent report of the Harvard Kennedy School on <u>The State and Fate of Community Banking</u>,

> *"Dodd-Frank will increase total U.S. financial regulatory restrictions thirty-two percent relative to 2010 levels once all of its rulemakings are complete. The legal costs for community banks associated with more regulations are inherently a larger portion of overall revenue than for larger institutions, making any form of compliance more difficult".*

In 2014, Bloomberg Global Economics reported on declining US worker productivity resulting from weak business investment, with corporate investment falling 25% in the years following the financial crisis, despite very low borrowing costs for US businesses. The reduced levels of equipment, software and building structures has left workers without the capital infrastructure needed to be more productive[205].

While the Fed's policies may have done little to bolster employment or wages, their policies have unquestionably resulted in lower mortgage rates. While the Fed's programs are credited with having spurred a boom in the refinancing of residential mortgages, the tightening credit standards of lenders and regulatory agencies that have accompanied this activity have rendered many borrowers unqualified. Hence, the savings from home mortgage refinancing have primarily benefited those with the highest credit scores and the greatest income qualifications, the wealthy. Moderate income homeowners and, of course, renters have derived no benefit whatsoever from lower mortgage rates. In fact, rents in most markets around the country have risen in the years following the financial crisis, in many cases quite dramatically.

While corporations and banks alike have seen their cost of borrowing fall precipitously, banks by and large have been unwilling to pass these savings on to consumers through lower interest rates on credit card balances and consumer loans. Banks, who have been able to borrow at interest rates near zero and have paid less than 1% of interest on consumer deposits for the past six years, have held credit card rates near their all-time high. Data of the Board of Governors of the Federal Reserve in a 2012 report to Congress on trends in bank credit card pricing found that average bank rates had fallen from 14.68% in the period leading up to the recession to just 13.09% by 2011. At the same time, the average return on assets of large US credit card banks had climbed from 2.75% in 2007 to 5.25% by 2011[206]. With the funding costs of banks near zero for this period and the interest rates charged on consumer loan balances at 13%, it's quite shocking that returns on bank assets weren't far higher!

At the same time, low corporate borrowing rates and an economy flush with excess liquidity courtesy of the Fed, have fueled dramatic gains in US stock prices. Over the period 2009-2013 the Dow Jones Industrial Average has more than doubled. In 2013, the Dow and the S&P 500 posted their largest gains in eighteen years. While rising stock prices favor all holders of equities, the gains are proportionate to the segments of society with the greatest ownership of stocks, in this case again, the wealthy. According to the Economic Policy Institute, roughly 60% of stock wealth is held by the top 1% of US households, measured by wealth. Roughly 80% of stock market gains go to the top 10% of American households[207].

The Reason Foundation in 2012 found that QE *"is fundamentally a regressive redistribution program…it is a primary driver of income inequality[208]."* By mid-2013, the Fed calculated that 91% of Americans' wealth in total had been recovered from the onset of the financial crisis, yet the wealth of the *average* US household had declined by more than half. This points out the unevenness of the recovery and the weighting of stocks and home ownership toward the aggregate wealth data. The Fed data attributes two-thirds of the gains to appreciating stock prices, a factor they acknowledge disproportionally favors the wealthy.

It is also worth mentioning that the Fed's policies of easy money may actually be harming the economy and postponing rather than promoting, true economic growth. One of the principal goals of the Bernanke Fed had been, in large part, the mitigation of the risk of price deflation in the economy, a particular concern of Ben Bernanke's and the underpinning of the Bernanke Doctrine. That Doctrine, following Bernanke's famous speech on the topic in 2002 argues that deflation can *always* be controlled under a monetary policy that increases the money supply, ensures liquidity in the financial system, lowers interest rates and devalues the dollar.

The Fed's strategy was, in part, to reduce the cost of capital to incentivize businesses to borrow for new capital expansion. New investment would spur new employment and thereby boost consumer spending and (modest) price inflation. The trouble is, now six years into the plan little of this has actually come about. Business investment has been lackluster, as has hiring, consumer spending has barely budged and inflation is still well below the Fed's target.

This raises the natural question of whether or not the Bernanke Doctrine is an economic *principle* or merely *speculation* and whether the Fed, through its monetary policy alone can effectively influence the demand for goods and services within the economy. Easy money, particularly coupled with a tough regulatory environment (as anyone will confirm who has applied for a loan) may actually serve to boost the *supply* of goods and services within the economy, with little or no impact upon aggregate *demand*. If this is the case, then easy monetary policy actually serves to promote deflation, and the Fed is in effect fighting itself. This would also explain the mystery of why the vast majority of the reserves the Fed has created through its multi-year policy of quantitative easing remain parked on the balance sheets of member banks, rather than in the hands of the public. If this is, in fact, an accurate assessment of the net effect of monetary policy at present, then there is little to support rising wages.

By 2012, the top 5% of Americans by income earned 22% of total US annual income, a figure that has risen steadily since 1975, when the share going to the top five percent was "only" 16%. Meanwhile, the share of *total income gains* over the period 2005 to 2012 captured by the wealthiest 20% of Americans by income was in excess of 60%. The lowest 40% received just over 6.5% of these gains[209].

Not surprisingly in this environment, as in the many years prior to the great recession, savings rates remain depressed. From levels of 10-13% of national income throughout the 1960s and 1970s, the US savings rate began a three-decade long decline beginning in the 1980s, falling to as low as 2.5% in the period prior to the financial crisis[210]. This long decline in the savings rate paralleled the stagnation in median family income over this period. With no real income growth, it remained difficult for people to increase their savings. It is also of great misfortune for us all, that this was the same period of time that a generation of families were charged with picking up the mantle for retirement savings, through the adoption and widespread implementation of 401(k) retirement savings plans.

There's one other point regarding retirement planning that's worth mentioning. With greater life expectancies and the demographic pyramid that historically provided the underpinning of Social Security and other defined benefit retirement plans now turned upside down, perhaps our most fundamental understanding of pension funding needs to be reexamined. The very notion that the government through payroll deductions, employers through annual contributions, or private individuals through tax-deferred savings plans could accumulate the resources necessary to fund America's retirement is in question.

Perhaps the better question to ask is why would we be so convinced that these alternatives *could* work? Maybe one answer, and arguably the only answer, is because they seemed to work just fine for the prior generation. A generation whose retirement funding bore no system legacy costs, whose retirement was often covered by defined-benefit employer plans and for whom the successive generation paying into the plans was far larger in numbers. A generation prior, who also never saw the retirement benefit increases in the public sector anywhere close to those successfully negotiated by public employee labor unions over the past twenty years.

The facts and circumstances concerning the prior generations and those now entering retirement are quite different. More to the point, something clearly has to be done *now* to prevent an impending disaster in elderly care in the years ahead. But perhaps tweaking the existing structures that had been cobbled together in a very different time and under very different circumstances is not the answer. The confluence of cataclysmic outcomes for Social Security, disappearing employer-sponsored defined benefit plans, deeply burdened public employee retirement systems and grossly underfunded 401(k)/IRAs can't simply be a coincidence.

*   *   *

We must also consider what is practical and what is not. We cannot save our way out of a problem that began long ago and that entered a critical phase when the first wave of Baby Boomers entered retirement in 2011. Given where we are today in providing for the daily retirement of the Baby Boom generation, Social Security is not only the best alternative, it is the *only* alternative for addressing America's retirement crisis.

Any attempts to shore up retirement funding for those entering or about to enter retirement through a savings plan, as has been proposed by Senator Harkin's Committee on Retirement, or by President Obama's myRA, are simply not possible. Not for this generation. A savings plan is premised on three critical variables: regular contributions, positive rates of return, and the compounding of returns *over time*. Senator Harken's USA Retirement Accounts and President Obama's myRA - great plans were they presented to Congress twenty years ago - fail on one of the most critical variables of a successful retirement plan, the element of time.

America's retirement crisis is immediate and the only path to solving it lies in changing the paradigm of Social Security, its purpose, its funding support and its value to society. We need to drop the flawed concept of Social Security benefits being an earned entitlement or governmental dividend for those who have paid into the system, as well as the equally erroneous view of Social Security as a partial supplement to elderly support for everyone. We need to begin to see Social Security in a manner that, it turns out, is actually far more consistent with its originally intended purpose: a safety net for America's elderly and disabled. In so doing, we must begin to think of Social Security as a policy goal of a civilized society, one that is no more capable of tolerating elderly poverty, than America was eighty years ago when the Social Security Act was drafted.

We must also delink our perception of the system from one that is self-funded, self-contained and earned, in favor of viewing Social Security as a critical social benefit, like education, science, medical research and national defense. Each of these programs are vital, consume a sizeable share of the federal budget, yet none are linked to a dedicated self-supported tax. In fact, many developed countries throughout the world, including Australia whose Age Pension system (the Australian version of Social Security) is ranked among the most successful retirement systems in the world, are financed just this way, with funding coming from general revenues, rather than a dedicated tax[211].

Second, Social Security benefits, for those qualifying, need to be substantially raised. A recent survey by the National Academy of Social Insurance of 2,000 Americans aged twenty-one and older showed that 84% of those polled believe that current Social Security benefits do not provide enough income for retirees. Seventy-five percent of respondents supported raising Social Security benefits and 87% would support higher taxes to preserve Social Security for the future[212].

A research study by prominent economist Dean Baker in 2011 pointed out that more than 75% of Social Security benefits are paid to people with less than $20,000 per year of other income[213]. If these benefits serve for many retirees as a near or entire means of support, then providing benefits at or below the poverty line, as is currently the practice, is not a reasonable solution to elderly care. Benefits need to be increased to bring people closer to median national income, or two to three times the current level of benefits for single-household recipients.

Third, we should eliminate the taxation of Social Security benefits instituted by Congress through passage of the Social Security Amendments of 1983 (H.R. 1900). For the forty-eight years preceding H.R. 1900, benefit payments were tax-exempt. Under budget pressure in the early 1980s (and also amidst the questionable self-dealing of broadening coverage of the system to employees of the Federal government - including all members of Congress, the President, Vice President and other executive level appointments) Congress moved to pass H.R. 1900 and to capture additional revenue to fund the Social Security Trust Fund, by taxing benefits. Of course Congress, with its additional federal employee coverages then in place and added tax revenue provided by this new tax, did not hesitate to quickly "borrow" back all excesses of the Trust Fund in subsequent years, with the monies redirected to other, non-retirement governmental programs.

Fourth, withdrawals from IRA and 401(k) plans in retirement for those with modest accounts, should also be exempt from taxation. If the median balance of those with retirement accounts in the country is currently $59,000, and this balance is supposed to provide a basis for support for twenty or thirty years, then it hardly makes sense for withdrawals from these accounts to be taxed. Taxes should be scaled in for withdrawals above a fair and reasonable annual threshold.

Now many reading this will immediately dismiss this whole idea of Social Security reform as a reckless use of government resources, providing the potential to blow a giant hole in the federal budget for years to come. This is not to say that these reforms should occur in a vacuum, without substantial review of the internal policies, programs and efficiencies of the Social Security Administration. The Administration's own financial report for fiscal year 2013 identifies some $1.7 billion in improper overpayments to individuals. These payments, representing a relatively small percentage of the Administration's total outlays, are typically recovered at only pennies on the dollar. But also consider this, in a handful of years Bill Gates and Larry Ellison will be eligible for Social Security benefits. Warren Buffet currently qualifies. Why? Because there is no means testing of benefits. And why not? Because we continue to view Social Security as an entitlement rather than a safety net for those who need it most.

Means testing of benefits is supported by numerous public interest groups, including the American Association of Retired People or ARRP. A thoughtful proposal on this issue was put forth by the American Academy of Actuaries in 2002[214]. By means testing benefits, we would greatly limit our exposure to Social Security benefits now and into the future. Adjustment would also need to be made for dual recipients of Social Security benefits within a given household. With an enhanced level of benefits, payments could be scaled in a way that many retirees of modest means would see no change in their Social Security benefits, while those who rely on the payments more heavily would be provided greater assistance. And Mr. Buffet? Sorry, but he'll be just fine without them.

Next, the current ceiling on wages subject to the FICA tax should be eliminated. For tax year 2015, the maximum taxable compensation subject to Social Security taxes will be $118,500. IRS data for the year 2012, however, shows just under 21 million individual tax returns, or 22% of the total taxable returns filed, with adjusted gross income of greater than $200,000. A total of 392,850 returns filed showed adjusted gross income of greater than $1,000,000. For these individuals, upwards of 90% of their income is exempt from the FICA tax. How is this reasonable? Were Social Security viewed as a *social benefit* and not as a retirement entitlement, there is no valid reason why there should be any cap on Social Security wages. Putting a cap on Social Security wages is nothing more than a massive tax break for the wealthy. This practice stems, once again, from the mistaken notion that Social Security benefits are earned. If FICA wages are not capped, then won't someone end up paying far more into the system than they receive in benefits? Yes, absolutely. But as the courts firmly established in Flemming v. Nestor, Social Security benefits are not a contractual right.

We must also consider that if the net effect of these changes is ultimately to increase the Federal budget deficit, then so be it. Funding elderly care becomes a much broader issue than simply measuring the impact of changes to one social program, amidst a broad range of federal expenditures that are otherwise simply assumed. In other words, if elderly care is as reasonable a social goal as national defense, education, transportation and the like, then the budget should be managed relative to our ability to provide for each of these expenditures. Once again, with the unique exception of Social Security, none of these other social benefit programs have any dedicated tax or premise of self-funding.

We must also consider that fiscal deficits provide economic stimulus. Former Chairman of the Federal Reserve Bank, Ben Bernanke, amidst a long list of renowned economists have been quite vocal in recent years about the limited ability of monetary policy alone to reinvigorate the US economy following the financial crisis. Bernanke, Nobel Laureates Paul Krugman, Joseph Stiglitz and other economists advocated then, as they do now, that Congress should provide some form of fiscal response (i.e., additional federal spending) to provide economic incentives. Deficit spending creates that stimulus and it really doesn't matter if the expenditures added are for public works programs or aid to seniors. Further, we must bear in mind that the enhanced Social Security benefits will largely be spent by retirees in their entirety on food, shelter, clothing and the like. Hence, these sales will drive tax revenue at the local level in the form of sales taxes, and also at the federal level in the form of incremental personal and corporate income tax for the businesses that prosper by the increased consumption. Hence, a considerable portion of the added federal subsidies under a reformed Social Security program would flow back to the Treasury as tax revenue.

Lastly, higher social security benefits for seniors would also reduce their current reliance on other government subsidies like food stamps and public assistance. Over four million low income adults over age sixty are enrolled in the Supplemental Nutrition Assistance Program (or SNAP, the official name for the food stamp program) while an estimated three out of five seniors who qualify simply do not apply[215]. With an average monthly allowance of $113 and four million recipients, SNAP payments to senior citizens amounted to nearly $5.5 billion in 2012. So in part, the budget impact of raising social security benefits may be muted by a corresponding decrease in other governmental assistance programs, like SNAP.

* * *

What may turn out to be the thornier problem for America is what in the heck to do about its public employee pension funding. For those cities who have filed for bankruptcy in an effort to resolve excessive pension and other costs, the courts have shown a willingness to treat pension beneficiaries more favorably than bondholders or other creditors of the local government. And maybe this is the lesson to be learned; that it's okay not to repay those who lend you money to build courthouses, police stations and other public projects, but wrong to default on promised pension benefits to retirees. Perhaps this will turn out to be the future of American local government finance. But this approach can only go so far.

First, and perhaps most immediate is the fact that states, unlike cities, counties and local districts cannot seek protection under Chapter 9 or any other section of the US bankruptcy laws. For those states like Illinois, New Jersey and Kentucky there is no quick fix to discharge obligations by placing the matter in the hands of friendly courts. These states are challenged greatly by their abilities to pay existing obligations and operating expenses, while also facing staggering levels of underfunded pension liabilities. They will either need to restructure their obligations outside of the bankruptcy process or seek to have the US bankruptcy laws revised.

Just such an effort has been proposed in addressing the debt and pension burdens of the island of Puerto Rico. A US commonwealth, the island state's government on June 28, 2014 passed the Puerto Rico Corporations Debt Enforcement and Recovery Act (the "Recovery Act") a measure designed to allow the island to restructure its *$70 billion* in public debts under a new local bankruptcy law, intended to parallel those provisions of Chapter 9 of the US Bankruptcy Code. A US federal judge, however, ruled in February of 2015 that the law violated the US constitution, which prohibits a state government from modifying its municipal debt. The commonwealth is now appealing the ruling and has introduced a bill in Congress to modify Chapter 9 of the US Bankruptcy Code.

While as a constitutional matter this latter approach is likely not possible for Puerto Rico or for any US state, any more so than it would be for the Federal government, unlike the Federal government the states do not have the power to print new currency as a way to meet unfunded obligations.

Second, for those cities that have resolved their immediate funding crises by petitioning the courts in bankruptcy, the relief may turn out to be only temporary. Without addressing the underlying fundamental issues that impact these cities' budgets, their emergence from bankruptcy court may be nothing more than a stopgap, temporary measure to keep creditors from their door. These cities will once again have new capital projects and infrastructure repairs that will need to be financed, but will find access to capital difficult, and investors unwilling to make the same mistakes twice.

At the same time, without addressing their growing pension burdens for current employees, local governments will find themselves deeper and deeper in the red, buried under overwhelming future liabilities. Current pension costs will consume an increasing portion of their general fund budgets, rendering services to residents unaffordable and impaired. Where permitted by state law, some will raise tax rates. Many will levy new charges for services like trash hauling that may have been otherwise covered under the general tax levy. Others will raise permitting and licensing fees, violations and citations, each as an end run on tax increases. Other will have no choice but to raise tax rates or create new taxes.

The State of California has recently proposed just this: a new broad sales tax on services. Previously untaxed services for accountants, legal fees, haircuts, gardening services, movie tickets, pest control and other items would now be subject to a services sales tax, projected to raise an additional $10 billion per year for the state. While proponents and opponents will argue over how the new revenue will be spent, ultimately, it doesn't matter. Public agencies often attempt to tie tax increases to programs with great public support like schools and health care, in an effort to gain voter support for the tax increase. But in the final analysis, these "dedicated" taxes often simply relieve the public agency of an existing budgetary obligation, thereby freeing up funds in the budget for less voter friendly purposes, like funding pensions.

Beyond the state-wide sales tax measure in California, 140 local government ballot measures are scheduled for the November 2015 election seeking to raise added tax revenue in the state, including new taxes on everything from soda to marijuana dispensaries. But any such measure that attempts to raise tax revenue will ultimately fall squarely on the backs of its residents, already suffering stagnant incomes, amidst the burden of paying daily expenses and the cost of funding their own retirement plans.

Several states have taken action in recent years to address the funding imbalances of their public employee retirement systems. Others like Wisconsin, Washington and South Dakota have reasonably high funded ratios. While states and local governments across the nation are seeking to modify retirement benefits for public employees, virtually all of these measures are prospective as to new employee hires. In fact, many state constitutions like that of New York State, where Governor Cuomo advocated public pension reforms in 2012, require that any amendments be applied only to new entrants to the system. From the 1938 New York State Constitution (Article V, Section 7):

"After July first, nineteen hundred forty, membership in any pension or retirement system of the state or of a civil division thereof shall be a contractual relationship, the benefits of which shall not be diminished or impaired."

Migrating new employees to 401(k) accounts, much the way Corporate America did in the 1980s may ease the funding burden of local governments in the future, but at the risk of dumping these new hires into the same quagmire that surrounds so many private sector workers today. Be that as it may, with existing public sector employees and current retirees in most states exempted from these changes, the benefits local governments seek to realize will not begin to impact their budgets for another 20-30 years.

This is certainly true of the Oklahoma Retirement Freedom Act, the 2014 pension reform measure undertaken in the State of Oklahoma. Beginning in November of 2015, Oklahoma state employees will be required to enter a 401(k) style retirement plan, following plan changes similarly enacted in Michigan and Alaska. Optional 401(k) style public employee retirement plans have also been put in place in Colorado, Montana, North Dakota, Ohio, Florida and South Carolina.

But the new plan in Oklahoma makes no changes to the existing defined benefit plan in effect for current and retired employees of the state. Furthermore, even future hires in the areas of firefighting and law enforcement will continue to be covered by the state's historical defined benefit plan.

These are important changes for the future, but will do little to address the state's $11 billion unfunded pension liability, a number that will almost certainly grow larger in the years ahead. And, as with all the public employee defined benefit plans we've discussed, unfunded liabilities will grow exponentially if the current high dependence on stock investments in public employee retirement systems suddenly turns sour, due to a sharp or prolonged downturn in the equities markets.

Perhaps the most interesting departure from this catch-22 of only being able to modify plan terms for new hires is the pension reform in Rhode Island, ushered in by then State Treasurer Gina Raimondo (subsequently elected Governor of the state in 2014). Rhode Island's pension legislation, unlike that of most other pension reform measures, actually reduces pension benefits for *current* workers as well as new hires. Among other changes, the legislation would increase the retirement age to sixty-seven from its current sixty-two. It would also suspend all further cost of living increases until the plan achieves a funded ratio of at least 80%. The legislation will also shift all workers (other than public safety) to a hybrid plan incorporating a defined contribution component. It is estimated that these plan changes have saved the state and its local governments a total of $400 million in 2014 (an amount equal to 11% of the state's annual tax revenue collections).

Ms. Raimondo, a Democrat and former venture capitalist, campaigned for the Governor's office in November 2014 and won largely on the basis of her success pushing through the Rhode Island Retirement Security Act of 2011, overcoming strong union opposition to the candidate and the Act. Undeterred by the losses in the legislature and at the polls, the public employee unions in Rhode Island have fought to challenge the matter in the courts ever since. Ms. Raimondo has sought to negotiate a settlement with the unions that was reported to have preserved 94% of the legislation's cost savings, but the deal ultimately fell through, despite approval from 70% of the employees who cast ballots for the settlement[216].

Recognizing the urgency of addressing its unfunded pension liabilities, the State of Kentucky legislature undertook a comprehensive bi-partisan review of its retirement systems in 2013. The plan involves the creation of a new retirement plan for workers hired after January 1, 2014, including a cash balance investment plan, a measure that is typical of most "hybrid" pension reform measures to date. Under the Kentucky plan, cost of living adjustments can only be provided to the extent they can be paid. If this change applies only to future (i.e., post January 1, 2014) enrollees in the plan, however, it will have a muted impact on the state's unfunded liabilities.

The Kentucky plan also commits the legislature to fully fund its annual pension obligations for all years going forward (in contrast to prior practice that in large part created the state's pension underfunding). It's questionable, though, as to the circumstances under which this provision may be amended by future legislatures. Generally speaking, the powers of one legislature to bind that of a future legislature are expressly limited. And lastly, the legislation provides for raising $100 million annually to help amortize the state's unfunded pension liability, although the source for this revenue, while unspecified and left to a future budget act, can only be taxes.

As if its public employee retirement system weren't enough to drive a migraine into the head of every state legislator, the Kentucky Teachers' Retirement System is suffering its own funding debacle, with assets totaling just 53% of what is expected to be needed to fund the retirement of an additional 141,000 school teachers, public university and state educational agency employees and retirees. New accounting rules going into effect in 2015 will nearly double the system's liabilities to $23 billion, reducing its funded status to 45%[217]. To address its latest (and seemingly never-ending) pension imbalance, the Speaker of the House, Greg Stumbo proposed legislation in early 2015 that would authorize the State to borrow $3.3 billion in bonds to shore up the teachers retirement system. While the addition of these funds will help shore up the underfunded status of the plan, the added debt service on $3.3 billion of bonds will, of course, further stress the states' operating budget.

So how is the State of Kentucky's lauded pension reform now working? Despite the efforts of the Kentucky legislature to bring forth substantive pension reform in 2013, new problems of the Kentucky Employees Retirement

System began to emerge by 2014 – just one year later. To address lower investment returns and revised assumptions on mortality rates covering an estimated 130,000 active and retired public employees, the retirement plan is now only 21% funded and is estimated to require another $95 million per year contribution from the state legislature[218].

* * *

ABOUT THE AUTHOR

R ichard DeProspo is an investment banker with over 30 years' experience assisting state and local governments throughout the country
with the financing of complex public projects. An expert on public employee
pension management, he has lectured widely on the topic and advised numerous municipalities and public pension funds nationwide on the proper
management of employee retirement liabilities. Mr. DeProspo holds B. A.
and M.B.A. degrees from the State University of New York and has been a
FINRA licensed securities professional serving municipal governments since
1980. He lives in Los Angeles, California with his family.

NOTES

1   "Social Security Fund to Run Out in 2035, Trustees Say",Bloomberg News April 23, 2012

2   "How America Saves 2014", Vanguard, June 13, 2014.

3   Consumer Finances 2010-2014, Federal Reserve Bulletin, Sept 2014.

4   "The Continuing Retirement Savings Crisis", by Nari Rhee, PhD and Ilana Boivie, March 2015

5   "401(k)/IRA Holdings in 2013: An Update from the SCF", Alicia Munnell, Center for Retirement Research, Sept 2014

6   2014 Retirement Confidence Survey, Employee Benefit Research Institute, March 2014

7   "Fidelity Estimates Couples Retiring in 2013 Will Need $220,00 to Pay Medical Expenses Throughout Retirement", Fidelity Investments, May 15, 2013

8   "The Retirement Savings Crisis: Is it Worse than we Think?", Nari Rhee, National Institute on Retirement Security, June 2013

9   "Number of Americans Reporting No Personal or Retirement Savings Rises", Harris Report February 2, 2011

10   "401(k) Plan Asset Allocation, Account Balances, and Loan Activity in 2013", Employee Benefit Research Institute, No. 408, December 2014

11   Interest.com Study, October 9, 2014, as reported by CNBC

12   "The Continuing Retirement Savings Crisis", by Nari Rhee, PhD and Ilana Boivie, March 2015

13   Gallup Annual Economy and Personal Finance Survey, 2014

14   "401(k) Plans in 2010: An Update from the SCF", Center for Retirement Research, Boston College, July 2012, Number 12-13

15   "2013 Retirement Confidence Survey" Employee Benefit Research Institute, March 2013.

16 "Cashing out can Derail Retirement: Employees in Transition Need Help", Fidelity Investments accessed at https://workplace.fidelity.com/resources/cost-cashing-out.html

17 "The Crisis in Pensions and Retirement Plans" Accounting Degree Review http://www.accounting-degree.org/retirement/

18 Federal Reserve Bank, 2013 Survey of Consumer Finance

19 "The Retirement Factor: The Role of Defined Benefit Pensions in Reducing Elder Economic Hardships", Porell and Oakley, National Institute for Retirement Security, July 2013

20 "The Hidden Fees in the 401(K)", Darryl Preston, Bloomberg Markets, March 2008

21 "The Retirement Savings Crisis: Is it Worse than we Think?", Nari Rhee, National Institute on Retirement Security, June 2013

22 "The Lifecycle of Spending; Retirement Insights" J. P. Morgan, January 2014.

23 "Population Aging Will Dampen Economic Growth over the Next Two Decades", Moody's Investors Service, August 6, 2014.

24 "World Population Prospects: The 2012 Revision", United Nations, Department of Economic and Social Affairs.

25 2015 Milliman Pension Funding Index, http://us.milliman.com/Solutions/Products/Pension-Funding-Index/

26 "The Sources of State and Local Tax Revenues", by Liz Malm and Elen Kant, the Tax Foundation. http://taxfoundation.org/article/sources-state-and-local-tax-revenues

27 "Public vs. Private Employees on the Pension Crisis: Nobody Wants Responsibility", by Emily Ekins, The Reason Foundation, February 9, 2015 www.reason.com

28 "History of Pension Plans", Employment Benefit Research Institute, March 1998

29 "Historical Background and Development of Social Security", Social Security Administration, http://www.ssa.gov/history/briefhistory3.html

30 Ibid.

31 Ibid.

32 Ibid.

33 "Research Note #17: The Townsend Plan's Pension Scheme", Social Security Administration, ssa.gov/history/townsendproblems.html

34 "Support of the Elderly Before the Depression: Individual and Collective Arrangements" by Carolyn L. Weaver, The Cato Institute,

35 "The Crisis in Pensions and Retirement Plans" Accounting Degree Review http://www.accounting-degree.org/retirement/

36 "Is the Social Security Trust Fund Solvent" Patton, Forbes, June 12, 2013

37 "Pervasive Medicare Fraud Proves Hard to Stop", New York Times, August 15, 2014.

38 The Department of HHS Health Care Fraud and Abuse Report for FY 2013

39 "US Sues NYC, Computer Sciences for alleged Medicaid Fraud" Reuters, Oct 27, 2014.

40 "Pervasive Medicare Fraud Proves Hard to Stop", New York Times, August 15, 2014.

41 www.hhs.gov/about

42 "An Update to the Budget and Economic Outlook: 2014 to 2024" CBO, August 27, 2014

43 "Covered Workers and Beneficiaries." United States Social Security Administration, Office of the Chief Actuary

44 2013 Agency Financial Report, Social Security Administration.

45 "Unfit for Work; the Startling Rise of Disability in America", Chana Joffe-Walt, NPR, 2014

46 "2014 Annual Social Security and Medicare Trust Fund Report", Social Security Administration

47 "Social Security Administration: Cases of Federal Employees and Transportation Drivers and Owners Who Fraudulently and/or Improperly Received SSA Disability Payments." United States Government Accountability Office, June 25, 2010

48 "The Sharp Rise In Disability Claims" John Merline, Region Focus, Richmond Federal Reserve Bank, Second/Third Quarter 2012

49 "The Impact of Unemployment Insurance Extensions on Disability Insurance Applications and Allowance Rates" Matthew Rutledge, Center for Retirement Research, Boston College Oct 2011

50 "Why Welfare Reform Has Failed", Peter Edelman Barbara Ehrenreich, Washington Post Op-ed, Dec 6, 2009

51 "Fidelity Estimates Couples Retiring in 2013 will need $220,000 to Pay Medical Expenses throughout Retirement", Fidelity Benefits Consulting, Fidelity.com May, 15, 2013

52 "The Disappearing Defined Benefit Pension and Its Potential Impact on the Retirement Incomes of Baby Boomers", Barbara A. Butrica, Howard

M. Iams, Karen E. Smith and Eric J. Toder, Social Security Bulletin, Vol 69 No. 3, 2009

53 "A Summary of the 2014 Annual Reports" Social Security and Medicare Boards of Trustees 2014

54 "Social Security: Follow the Math" by Michael D. Tanner, the Cato Institute, January 14, 2005

55 "Social Security Facts" James Agresti and Stephen Cardone, Just Facts, January 27, 2011

56 "Misconceptions and Realities About Who Pays Taxes" by Chuck Marr and Chye-Ching Huang, Center on Budget and Policy Priorities, September 17, 2012 http://www.cbpp.org/cms/?fa=view&id=3505#_ftnref15

57 The 2014 Annual Report of the Board of Trustees of the Federal Old-Age and Survivors Insurance and Federal Disability Insurance Trust Funds

58 "Period Life Expectancy." United States Social Security Administration, Office of the Chief Actuary.

59 "Is the Social Security Trust Fund Solvent" Patton, Forbes, June 12, 2013

60 "Social Security Fund to Run Out in 2035, Trustees Say", Bloomberg News, April 24, 2012

61 "History Suggests Social Security Insolvency is coming Sooner Than Projected", Rachel Greszler, The Heritage Foundation, June 27, 2013.

62 Social Security Administration. http://www.ssa.gov/OACT/progdata/fundFAQ.html#a0=2

63 "Social Security: Its Worse Than You Think", Gary King and Samir S. Soneji, New York Times, Jan 5, 2013

64 Ibid.

65 "401(k) /IRA Holdings in 2013: An Update From The SCF", by Alicia H. Munnell, Center for Retirement Research, September 2014, Number 14-15

66 "FAQs About Benefits - Retirement Issues: What are the trends in US retirement plans?" http://www.ebri.org/publications/benfaq/index.cfm?fa=retfaq14

67 "The Continuing Retirement Savings Crisis", by Nari Rhee, PhD and Ilana Boivie, National Institute on Retirement Security, March 2015

68 "The Retirement Savings Crisis: Is it Worse than we Think?", Nari Rhee, National Institute on Retirement Security, June 2013

69 "A Giant Falls: The Bankruptcy of General Motors", The Economist, June 4, 2009

70 "What Explains GM's Problems with the UAW?", Doug Altner, Forbes, May 20, 2013

71 "GM Won't Tackle Pension Talks with UAW Until 2015", Ben Klayman, Reuters, September 27, 2013.

72 "US Government Says it Lost $11.2 Billion on GM Bailout", Reuters, April 30, 2014

73 "Silver City No More? Taunton's Reed & Barton Files for Bankruptcy", Charles Winokoor, Taunton Gazette, February 19, 2015. http://www. tauntongazette.com/article/20150219/NEWS/150216074/13406/NEWS

74 "United Air Wins Right to Default on its Employee Pension Plans", Maynard, New York Times, May 11, 2005

75 "The Disappearing Defined Benefit Pension and Its Potential Impact on Retirement" Butrica, Iams, Smith and Toder, Social Security Bulletin, Vol 69, NO 3, 2009

76 "Companies Prepare to Dump Pension Plans in 2014", Forbes, Mar 19, 2014

77 "Why the Pension Gap is Soaring", Vipal Monga, The Wall Street Journal, February 26, 2013

78 "The Last Private Industry Pension Plans", William J. Wiatrowski, BLS Monthly Labor Review, Dec 2012

79 "Feds Place 150 Union Pension Funds in 'Critical' Status" by Sean Higgins, Washington Examiner, February 1, 2015

80 "Fiscal 2013 Pension Medians: Adjusted Net Pension Liabilities", Moody's Investor Service, Nov 20, 2014

81 "Another $54 Billion?" by Jonathan Ingram, Illinois Policy, April 9, 2012, www.illinoispolicy.org/reports/another-54-billion-in-addition-to-pensions-the-state-owes-billions-more-in-retiree-health-benefits/

82 "Illinois is Running out of Time and Money", by George F. Will, April 25, 2012, The Washington Post

83 "Illinois Enters a State of Insolvency" by Paul Merrion, Greg Hinz and Steven Strahler, Crain's Chicago Business, January 16, 2010

84 "Why PERS Reform is Imperative in 2 Charts", Nevada Policy Research Institute December, 2014, http://www.npri.org/issues/publication/why-pers-reform-is-imperative-in-2-charts

85 "Retiring in the lap of Luxury: Nevada Government Pensions are often Better than Paychecks", by Victor Joecks and Robert Fellner, Nevada Policy Research Institute, January 22, 2015

86 "Controller John Chiang Drops Bombshell on California Public Pensions", Dan Walters, Sacramento Bee, Nov 01, 2014, http://www.sacbee.com/news/politics-government/dan-walters/article3507521.html

87 "No Escape from Pension Math in Pennsylvania", Bloomberg News, December 9, 2014

88 "Chicago: How Pensions Have Weakened the Credit Quality of America's Third Largest City", Moody's Investors Service, August 6, 2013

89 Chicago Police Benefit Fund Actuarial Report 2012

90 "Moody's Cuts Chicago Public Schools Rating to Baa3", Reuters, February 6, 2015, http://www.reuters.com/article/2015/03/07/usa-chicago-education-ratings-idUSnMDY8gZDg20150307

91 "Chicago: How Pensions Have Weakened the Credit Quality of America's Third Largest City", Moody's Investors Service, August 6, 2013

92 "Underfunded Public Pensions in the United States: The Size of the Problem, the Obstacles to Reform and the Path Forward", Thomas J. Healey, Carl Hess, Kevin Nicholson, Harvard Kennedy School, 2012

93 "Mayor's Proposal Calls for 7.5% Tax Hike: 2015 Lancaster Budget", Lancaster Online, http://lancasteronline.com/news/local, November 26, 2014

94 "Scranton Pensions Increased as much as 80 Percent", Terrie Morgan-Besecker, The Times-Tribune, December 14, 2014

95 "Auditor General Concerned About Underfunded State Pensions" by Sarah Arbogast, CBS Pittsburgh, June 6, 2014

96 "Fiscal 2013 Pension Medians: Adjusted Net Pension Liabilities", Moody's Investor Service, Nov 20, 2014

97 "Convicted Georgia Police Chief to Collect Pension in Prison", by Russ Bynum, the Associated Press, February 19, 2015

98 "Public Pension Plan Reform: the Legal Framework", Amy Monahan, University of Minnesota, Twin Cities School of Law, March 17, 2010

99 "No Clear Winner in Wisconsin's Summer of Discontent." O'Brien, Brendan and Mary Wisniewski *Reuters.* August 17, 2011

100 "Wisconsin Recall Breaks Records thanks to Outside Cash", Paul Abowd, The Center for Public Integrity, June 3, 2012

101 "Wisconsin Recall Breaks Records thanks to Outside Cash", Paul Abowd, The Center for Public Integrity, June 3, 2012

102 "Walker Survives Wisconsin Recall Vote", Davey, Zeleny, The New York Times, June 5, 2012

103 "A Liberal Mugged by Pension Reality" Allysia Finley, The Wall Street Journal, November 30, 2013

104 San Jose Fiscal Reforms, "About Measure B"

105 "Detroit Files Plan to Restructure, Leave Bankruptcy" Fox News, February 21, 2014

106 The Looting of Detroit's Pensions, Andrew G. Biggs, The American.

107 "Once Bankrupt Vallejo Still Can't Afford its Pricey Pensions", CNN Money, March 10, 2014

108 "United States Bankruptcy Court Eastern District of California, Opinion Regarding Confirmation and Status of CALPERS", Case No. 12-32118—9. February 4. 2015

109 "Broke California Cities Can Slice Pensions", by Steven Greenhut, U-T San Diego, February 11, 2015

110 "A New Chapter for Stockton: Post-Bankruptcy" by Roger Phillips, the Stockton Record, February 24, 2015, http://www.recordnet.com/article/20150224/NEWS/150229797

111 "Public Sector Pensions: How Well Funded are they, Really?", State Budget Solutions, Andrew G. Biggs, July 2012

112 2014 Report on State Retirement Systems: Funding Levels and Asset Allocation, Wilshire Consulting, February 26, 2014

113 Congressional Budget Office, "Estimating the Value of Subsidies for Federal Loans and Loan Guarantees," August 2004

114 "Dow 28,000,000: The Unbelievable Expectations of California's Pension System", David Crane, The Wall Street Journal, May 19, 2010.

115 LAPD Salaries, Los Angeles Times, August 6, 2010

116 "Police Chief's $204,000 Pension Shows How Cities Crashed", Bloomberg News, July 31, 2012

117 "Felon Fights for $540,000 Public Pension", Orange County Register, March 4, 2014

118 "Newport Lifeguards Swimming in Cash", The Orange County Register, May 10, 2011

119 City of Newport Beach Comprehensive Annual Financial Report, Fiscal Year Ended June 30, 2012

120 "Explosive Growth in CalPERS $100K Pension Club", Orange County Register, July 6, 2013.

121 "Big Pensions Drive Proposed Tax Increases on California Ballots", Mark Bucher, Sacramento Bee, October 25, 2014

122 State of Illinois Top 200 Government Pensions as of April 1, 2014. Taxpayers Educational Foundation http://dig.abclocal.go.com/wls/documents/Illinois%20pensions.pdf

123 "Oregon Public Employees Retirement System; Bellotti Pension Raises Bigger Questions", Jeff Mapes, November 26, 2011, he Oregonian gov. oregonlive.com.

124 Ballotpedia.org

125 "Nearly 5,000 Teachers Cashing in on Six-Figure Pensions", Leonard Greene, the New York Post, February 12, 2015.

126 "Nearly 8,000 State Workers Earn Pensions of More than $100,000 a Year", Michael Gormley, Newsday, March 10, 2015

127 EmpireCenter, http://www.empirecenter.org/wp-content/uploads/2015/02/NYCTRS-top100-2014.pdf

128 Legislative Issue Brief "Municipal Pension Reform", February 10, 2015, Florida League of Cities http://www.floridaleagueofcities.com/Assets/Files/Advocacy/2015_IB-PensionReform.pdf

129 "199 L.A. County Workers Made at Least $250,000 Last Year", Los Angeles Times, October 5, 2010.

130 "Pension Spiking may cost Phoenix $12 mil per Year", Craig Harris and Dustin Gardiner, The Arizona Republic, October 17, 2013.

131 "Pennsylvania Enacts Anti-Pension Spiking Provisions", Sam Rodriguez, Reason Foundation, January 10, 2014, http://reason.org/blog/show/pennsylvania-passes-anti-pension-sp.

132 "Governor McCrory Sings into La Measure to Curb Pension Spiking in NC", Dan Kane, Newobserver.com http://www.newsobserver.com/2014/07/30/4039936_mccrory-signs-into-law-measure.html?rh=1

133 "Cuomo Doing Nothing to end Pension Spiking", Post Editorial Board, October 26, 2013.

134 "Governor Cuomo Announces Passage of Major Pension Reform", March 15, 2012, New York State Governor's website http://www.governor.ny.gov/news/governor-cuomo-announces-passage-major-pension-reform

135 "Public Pension Spiking: No One's Monitoring Overtime Spiking in Minnesota", MaryJo Webster, Christopher Magan, Pioneer Press http://www.twincities.com/pensions/ci_22148781/public-pension-spiking-no-ones-monitoring-overtime-spiking

136 "Legal Pension Spiking will cost California $800 million, Audit Says", San Jose Mercury News, September 11, 2014.http://www.mercurynews. com/pensions/ci_26507597/legal-pension-spiking-will-cost-california- 800-million

137 "County CEO Steps Down as Colleagues Say Goodbye", Kathleen Wilson, Ventura County Star, March 22, 2011

138 "Salary Spiking Drains Public Pension Funds, Analysis Finds", Catherine Saillant, the Los Angeles Times, March 3, 2014

139 "Salary Spiking Drains Public Pension Funds, Analysis Finds", Catherine Saillant, the Los Angeles Times, March 3, 2014

140 "Judge Rules Controversial Ventura County Pension Reform Proposal Must be Removed from Ballot", KCLU, August 4, 2014

141 "1,223 Make More Than Malloy", Yankee Institute for Public Policy, February 19, 2013

142 "What They Make 2013-2014", Empire Center, July 23, 2014

143 Union Members Survey, US Bureau of Labor Statistics, Economic News Release, January 23, 2015, http://www.bls.gov/news.release/union2.nr0.htm

144 OpenSecrets.org, https://www.opensecrets.org/industries/indus.php?ind= P04

145 "The Trouble with Public Sector Unions", Daniel Disalvo, National Affairs, Issue Number 5, Fall 2010

146 "The State of State Pension Plans" Rachel Barkley, Morningstar, November 2012

147 "Nine States with Sinking Pensions", by Michael B. Sauter, Alexander E. M. Hess and Samuel Weigley, Yahoo Finance, November 8, 2012 http://finance.yahoo.com/news/nine-states-with-sinking-pensions.html

148 "The 80% Pension Funding Standard Myth", American Academy of Actuaries, Issue Brief, July 2012

149 "The Financial Crisis at the Kitchen Table: Trends in Household Debt" Brown, Haughwout, Lee and van der Klaauw, Federal Reserve Bank of New York, Vol 19, No. 2, 2013

150 "The Boom and Bust of US Housing Prices from Various Geographic Perspectives", Cohen, Coughlin and Lopez, Federal Reserve Bank of St. Louis Review, Sept/Oct 2012

151 "Don't Expect Consumer Spending to be the Engine of Economic Growth it Once Was" William R. Emmons, FRB St. Louis January 2012

152 "Underfunded Public Pensions in the United States: The Size of the Problem, the Obstacles to Reform and the Path Forward", Healey, Hess, Nicholson, Harvard Kennedy School Working Paper, 2012-08 based upon US Bureau of Economic Analysis data, www.bea.gov

153 "The Looting of Detroit's Pensions", by Andrew G. Biggs, February 16, 2014 American Enterprise Institute

154 "Underfunded Public Pensions in the United States: The Size of the Problem, the Obstacles to Reform and the Path Forward", Healey, Hess, Nicholson, Harvard Kennedy School Working Paper, 2012-08.

155 "New Front in Benefits Fight, Atlanta May Drop Pensions." McWhirter, Cameron and Belkin Douglas, *The Wall Street Journal.* June 22, 2011

156 Property Tax Update, Issue Brief 2012-207, the Florida Senate, September 2011

157 "Quarterly Summary of State and Local Government Tax Revenue", US Census Bureau June 29, 2010

158 Ballotpedia.org interview with Councilmember Pete Constant, June 11, 2013.

159 "California City Pension Burdens" by Marc Joffe, California Policy Center, February 17, 2015, http://californiapolicycenter.org/wp-content/uploads/2015/02/20150217_California-City-Pension-Burdens.pdf

160 "California is No Detroit", John D. R. Clark, Los Angeles Times, December 29, 2013

161 "Status Report of the New Jersey Pension and Health Benefits Study Commission", Sept 25, 2014

162 "Gauging the Spook Factor for Municipal Bond Investors" Michael Brooks, Alliance Bernstein, Oct 27, 2014

163 Kevyn Orr, *City of Detroit Proposal for Creditors*, June 14, 2013, http://s3.documentcloud.org/documents/713693/detroit-emergency-manager-kevyn-orrs-report-to.pdf

164 "LA Pension Agency Decision Deepens City's Budget Hole", Los Angeles Times, Oct 28, 2014

165 New Jersey Employers' Benefits and Pension Admin Manual, PERS Employer Pension Contribution Rates

166 "Judge Approves Stockton Bankruptcy Plan; Workers' Pensions Safe", Los Angeles Times, October 31, 2014

167 "California Pension Hikes Loom After CalPERS Vote" Reuters, Feb 18 2014

168 "As New Yorkers Live Longer, Cuomo Seeks Pension IOU", by Freeman Klopott, Bloomberg Business, February 13, 2015

169 "Seventy Percent of the FDNY's Females are Retiring on Disability" by Susan Edelman, the New York Post, February 22, 2015

170 "New York City Pension System Is Strained by Costs and Politics", by David W. Chen and Marky Williams Walsh, The New York Times, August 3, 2014

171 "Health Benefits are a Promise School Districts Find Hard to Keep", by Zahira Torres, the Los Angeles Times, March 7, 2015

172 "John Chiang: Numbers Reveal Unfunded Health Care Crisis", by John Chiang, Special to Sacramento Bee, January 3, 2015

173 Actuarial Valuation of Other Post-Employment Benefits Provided Under the Texas Employees Group Benefits Program, GSB Statement No. 43 for the Fiscal Year Ending August 31, 2014, Employees Retirement System of Texas

174 *"Diverging Trends Underlie Stable Overall U.S. OPEB Liability"*, Standard & Poor's (S&P) Rating Services, November 17, 2014

175 "Updating the Debate on Intergenerational Fairness in Pension Reform" Working Paper, Kenneth Howse, Oxford Institute of Ageing, March 2007

176 "200,000 Retired State Workers' Long Term Health Care Isn't Funded", San Francisco Chronicle, December 21, 2014

177 "UC's Pension Fiasco", Lawrence McQuillan, National Review Online WWW.NATIONALREVIEW.COM

178 Center for Retirement Research, September 2014, Number 14-15

179 "Employee Retirement Security Act", Wikipedia.

180 "History of 401(k) Plans" ERBI 2005

181 Center for Retirement Research, September 2014, Number 14-15

182 Center for Retirement Research, September 2014, Number 14-15

184 "The Path of Least Resistance in 401(k) Plans", Andrew Balls, National Bureau of Economic Research

183 Investment Company Institute, 2014

184 SPIVA US Scorecard, S&P Research, Year-end 2014

185 "A Look at 401(k) Fees" US Department of Labor publications.

186 "The Risks of Cashing Out Your 301(k) Early", Fidelity April 17, 2014

187 Center for Retirement Research, September 2014, Number 14-15

188 "Five Habits of 401(k) Millionaires", Fidelity Viewpoints, January 2, 2014, https://www.fidelity.com/viewpoints/retirement/how-to-become-a-millionaire-with-a-401(k)

189 "Why The Average Investor's Investment Return is So Low", Sean Hanlon, Forbes, April 24, 2014

190 Federal Reserve Bank, 2013 Survey of Consumer Finance

191   Consumer Finances 2010-2014, Federal Reserve Bulletin, Sept 2014

192   "Unlike the 1950s, there is no "typical" US family today", Brigid Schulte, The Washington Post, September 4, 2014

193   "The Retirement Crisis and a Plan to Solve it" US Senate Committee Report, July 2012

194   Social Security Administration website: http://www.ssa.gov/OACT/ progdata/fundFAQ.html#a0=2

195   "Pensions at a Glance 2013: OECD and G20 Indicators", Organization for Economic Cooperation and Development, 2014

196   US Census Bureau Report, Reuters, Sep 16, 2014

197   "Big US Firms Shift Hiring Abroad", The Wall Street Journal, April 19, 2011

198   "Income and Wage Gaps Across the US" Global Insight, US Conference of Mayors, August 2014

199 "Out of Work, Out of Options, Into Retirement" NBC News.com, Oct 13, 2009

200 "2013 Retirement Confidence Survey" Employee Benefit Research Institute, March 2013

201 "America's Wealth Gap Between Middle Income and Upper Income Families is Widest on Record", Richard Fry and Rakesh Kochhar, Per Research Center, December 17, 2014

202 "Don't Expect Consumer Spending to the Engine of Economic Growth It Once Was", William R. Emmons, Federal Reserve Bank of St. Louis, January 2012

203 "Investment Falls off a Cliff", Sudeep Reddy and Scott Thurm, The Wall Street Journal, November 19, 2012

204 "The State and Fate of Community Banking" by Marshall Lux and Robert Greene, Harvard Kennedy School, February 2015

205 "Companies Choose Profits Over Productivity", Matthew Phillips, Peter Coy, Bloomberg Business, May 15, 2014

206 Report to the Congress on the Profitability of Credit Card Operations of Depository Institutions" June 2012ß

207 "The State of Working America", 12th Edition, Economic Policy Institute, November 2012

208 "How Quantitative Easing Helps the Rich and Soaks the Rest of Us", Anthony Randazzo, the Reason Foundation, Sep 17, 2012

209 "Income and Wage Gaps Across the US" Global Insight, US Conference of Mayors, August 2012

210 Source: Federal Reserve Bank of St. Louis

211 "The Most Sustainable Pension Systems in the World", Allianz study, April 1, 2014, https://www.allianz.com/en/press/news/studies/news_2014-04-01.html

212 "Strengthening Social Security: What do Americans Want", National Academy of Social Insurance, 2013

213 "The Potential Savings to Social Security from Means Testing", Dean Baker and Hye Jin Rho, Center for Economic and Policy Research, March 2011

214 "Means Testing for Social Security", Issue Brief, American Academy of Actuaries, Dec 2012

215 Facts about SNAP and Senior Hunger, National Council on Aging, www.NCOA.org

216 "The Trial of a Democratic Pension Reformer", by Allysia Finley, The Wall Street Journal, September 4, 2014

217 "Stumbo Proposes $3.3 Billion Bond to prop up Kentucky Teachers' Retirement System", by John Cheves, Kentucky.com http://www.kentucky.com/2015/01/09/3632802/stumbo-proposes-33-billion-bond.html

218 "Pension Problems", Editorial, The Courier-Journal, December 8, 2014

www.ingramcontent.com/pod-product-compliance
Lightning Source LLC
Chambersburg PA
CBHW060545200326
41521CB00007B/493